Marginalized, Maligned & Miraculous Women in Scripture

Marginalized, Maligned & Miraculous

Women in Scripture

Deborah Spink Winters, Editor

JUDSON PRESS
PUBLISHERS SINCE 1824
VALLEY FORGE, PA

Judson Press has made every effort to trace the ownership of all quotes. In the event of a question arising from the use of a quote, we regret any error made and will be pleased to make the necessary correction in future printings and editions of this book.

Unless otherwise indicated, Bible quotations in this volume are from the New Revised Standard Version of the Bible, copyright © 1989 by the Division of Christian Education of the National Council of the Churches of Christ in the United States of America. Used by permission. All rights reserved. Other quotations are from *The Holy Bible*, King James Version; and from HOLY BIBLE, New International Version®, NIV®, copyright © 1973, 1978, 1984, 2011 by Biblica Inc. Used by permission. All rights ·
reserved worldwide.

Interior design by Crystal Devine.
Cover design by Wendy Ronga, Hampton Design Group.

Library of Congress Cataloging-in-Publication data

Cataloging-in-Publication Data available upon request.
Contact cip@judsonpress.com.

Printed in the U.S.A.

First printing, 2019.

Contents

Introduction

The birth of this book, *Marginalized, Maligned & Miraculous Women in Scripture*, took place in the midst of unveiling its predecessor, *Through Her Eyes: Bible Studies on Women in Scripture* (Judson Press, 2016). Many of the students who contributed to that first volume of Bible studies had gathered for our first book signing and a chance to talk about their chapters and how God had led us through the whole process. During that gathering, a gentleman came up to me and said, "Your book talks about twenty different biblical women. I had no idea there were twenty women in the Bible!" All of my students within earshot turned and looked at the man incredulously as I replied, "There are a lot more than twenty women in the Bible whose stories need to be heard." And hence this volume was born.

When my next Women in the Bible class met in Fall 2016, I asked them if they were interested in writing a second collection, with the stipulation that it could not contain any of the women who were in the original book. Their answer was a resounding *yes*!

Purpose

With the guidance of our editor, Rebecca Irwin-Diehl, the class agreed that the purpose of this book is to invite the reader to discover his or her own voice through the stories of the authors inspired by marginalized, maligned, and miraculous women of the Bible.

As a class we defined what each term meant to us:

Marginalized: unappreciated, overlooked, and deemed insignificant in society; voiceless, powerless, and devalued. Examples are widows, whose economic situation often was precarious (e.g., the widow of Zarephath), or women who were considered other or outsiders (e.g., the Canaanite woman who asked Jesus to heal her daughter).

Maligned: misjudged, vilified, abused, and belittled based on the perceptions of others. In this category is Hagar, the Egyptian slave woman who was treated cruelly by her jealous mistress, Sarai, when Hagar was pregnant with Abram's son Ishmael.

Miraculous: having overcome great odds by divine encounter or through divine enablement. These women include the daughters of Zelophehad, whose plea to Moses set a legal precedent, or Talitha-cumi, the little girl who was raised from the dead by Jesus after the mourners had sneered about such an impossibility.

These categories are somewhat arbitrary. By virtue of being female, all of the women would have been marginalized in their society and culture. Yet their appearance in the Bible suggests that most, if not all, of them had a divine interaction that might qualify them as miraculous (e.g., women were raised from the dead; God promised many descendants to Hagar). And even if they were not maligned in the biblical story, most of these women of Scripture have suffered in translation at some point in the Judeo-Christian tradition, if only through being overlooked and ignored for generations.

As we talked, we identified women in the Bible who are less well-known than, for example, Sarah, Rebekah, or Ruth, but whose stories resonated with us and deserve to be told.

Methodology

We also defined the methodology behind these volumes in what is known as narrative theology. Narrative theology recognizes the transformational power of story and metaphor (much like Jesus' use of parable) to teach and understand theology (God). When we start to take seriously God's story, also known as the metanarrative, and how we come to know God through the stories of the women in the Bible it gives us a framework with which to find meaning in our own life's story and to begin to see the hand of God in *our* lives. One of the greatest gifts you can give someone is the willingness to listen to his or her story. When we take the time to listen for God in someone else's story, what we learn can change our lives.

How to Use This Book

This book can be used as either a personal devotional book or as a small-group Bible study resource. This book is set up exactly as *Through Her Eyes* with one addition: based on feedback we received about that first volume, we added space for readers to make notes from their own private reflections of the chapter or from their small-group discussions.

The structure of the book guides readers through the content of the stories and through the process of listening and discernment. The book is set up as follows:

The Woman: the chapter title gives the name or brief identifying description of the biblical woman being studied.

Tagline: a one-line summation of something the story of the woman of Scripture has to teach us.

Quote: a brief quotation to focus the reader on an action or aspect of the biblical woman's character.

Hook Question(s): asks the reader to reflect on how he or she would respond to a given situation based on the life of the scriptural woman.

Biblical Story: the heart of the biblical story about the woman being studied, taken from the New Revised Standard Version and provided for the reader's convenience, along with other possible biblical references for their further study.

Biblical Exposition: a short explanation of the biblical setting and background of the story.

Personal Story: the author of the chapter reflects on how the biblical woman's story has touched her or his life.

Questions: posed for the reader to reflect on how the stories of the biblical woman and the author have touched the reader's life.

Thought for Your Day: a one-line sentence or phrase to focus a point that the material teaches.

Closing Prayer: provided for the reader to conclude the study, with the encouragement to go beyond the written prayer, trusting the Holy Spirit to guide as this material touches the reader's life.

Author's Biographical Information: a short blurb about each chapter author, given so that the reader has a better understanding of each contributor's personal story.

Connecting with Your Story: space for readers to make notes about their response to the story and the discussion in their Bible study.

For the Facilitator of Small-Group Studies

When using this book for small groups or study, I recommend reading through the entire chapter before presenting it to your small group. Ask the Holy Spirit to guide your preparation and to bless each person who will be studying with you.

This material is put together in such a way that it can be read during your small-group gathering. If possible, however, ask each member of your group to work through the chapter and each of the questions before coming to your group meeting. This will allow plenty of time for each participant to share answers to the questions and to discuss together how the material has touched their lives. I also strongly suggest three things for the group leader:

1. Pray before your small-group meeting, asking God to guide the discussion that needs to happen during your meeting between your members and trusting that the Holy Spirit will show up in your meeting.

2. At your first session, create your own group behavioral covenant, which will help make your group meeting a safe place for each of your participants to share at a deep level. (See the introduction from *Through Her Eyes* if you have never done a behavioral covenant before.) For more details about behavioral covenants, please see Gil Rendle, *Behavioral Covenants in Congregations: A Handbook for Honoring Differences* (Lanham, MD: Rowman and Littlefield, 1998), or http://images.acswebnetworks.com/1/498/IntroductiontoBehavioralCovenants.pdf.

3. Be willing to take the first step by sharing how each chapter has affected you. Be ready to share a personal story from your own life as God leads you to do so.

Begin each group meeting by having each participant, including you, answer the Hook Question for the chapter. Read the Biblical Text and Personal Story aloud (unless everyone has read it at home). You might also share a personal story from your life that relates to the biblical text.

Give each person the chance to answer the questions at the end of the chapter, inviting your introverted participants to exercise their voices but also permitting people to "pass" if they prefer. Always end your meeting with a devotional moment. This might involve reading the written closing prayer aloud in unison, or sharing a brief devotional based on the chapter's material and prepared in advance by you or another member of the group.

This volume is also set up so an individual or small group can work through the whole book at once or opt for a shorter, thematic study. For example, the book's content is organized to allow for a five-week study on the Marginalized, Maligned or Miraculous Women. Alternatively, a facilitator might tailor the content to create a shorter or longer study, selecting women of the Hebrew Scriptures or women of the Gospels, unnamed women or little-known women, and so on.

We have heard from individuals and small groups across the United States and from as far away as South Africa about how the original collection helped them to better understand how their stories intersect with the biblical text and God's story. We know that, as you work your way through this book, God will show up in your life and in the lives of your Bible study group members as well. If you have any suggestions on how to make this material more beneficial to you or your ministry setting, please let me know!

God bless,
Rev. Dr. Deborah Spink Winters
dwinters@eastern.edu
Summer 2018

Part One

Marginalized Women

Marginalized: unappreciated, overlooked, and deemed insignificant in society; voiceless, powerless, and devalued.

1

The Woman Caught in Adultery

Mercy Triumphs over Judgment

SOPHIA ALEXIS FOUTRES

*Most of us were taught that God would love
us if and when we change. In fact, God loves
you so that you can change. What empowers
change, what makes you desirous of change, is the
experience of love. It is that inherent experience
of love that becomes the engine of change.*
—Richard Rohr[1]

Hook Question

What if God's love for you really wasn't based on your
behavior?

Biblical Story: John 7:53–8:11

Then each of them went home, while Jesus went to the Mount
of Olives. Early in the morning he came again to the temple.
All the people came to him and he sat down and began to teach
them. The scribes and the Pharisees brought a woman who
had been caught in adultery; and making her stand before all

of them, they said to him, "Teacher, this woman was caught in the very act of committing adultery. Now in the law Moses commanded us to stone such women. Now what do you say?" They said this to test him, so that they might have some charge to bring against him. Jesus bent down and wrote with his finger on the ground. When they kept on questioning him, he straightened up and said to them, "Let anyone among you who is without sin be the first to throw a stone at her." And once again he bent down and wrote on the ground. When they heard it, they went away, one by one, beginning with the elders; and Jesus was left alone with the woman standing before him. Jesus straightened up and said to her, "Woman, where are they? Has no one condemned you?" She said, "No one, sir." And Jesus said, "Neither do I condemn you. Go your way, and from now on do not sin again."

Biblical Exposition

Many years ago, the biblical book of Exodus tells us that a man named Moses was given laws concerning the people from God. Ten especially important principles were written by the hand of God on two stones; these are most commonly known as the Ten Commandments. One of the laws insists, "You shall not commit adultery" (Exodus 20:14). In the Gospel of John, we find a story about adultery, one that was not included in the earliest manuscripts for various reasons; however, the story ultimately found its way into our biblical text and our hearts. I believe this story was questioned at first because it is one filled with surprising grace.

These twelve verses were woven in between stories of Jesus during his three years of active ministry on earth. In the previous chapter, at the culmination of an annual seven-day festival of the Jews remembering God's faithfulness, Jesus offered to slake the people's thirst and described the rivers of living water, which was the Spirit, that would flow from the hearts of the people who believed in his words (John

7:37-39). In the verses directly after the woman's story, Jesus promised the people that he would be light in their darkness. He exclaimed, "I am the light of the world. Whoever follows me will never walk in darkness but will have the light of life" (John 8:12).

Surrounded by promises of satisfaction and light, an unnamed woman was thrown at the feet of Jesus. The religious leaders, who were especially concerned with the laws, brought this woman to Jesus to test his faithfulness to the law. Everyone was well-informed about the commandment forbidding adultery, given generations earlier, and about the consequence that was required—stoning. This woman was caught in sin and was going to pay according to the religious people.

I found it amazing that Jesus did not even mention the woman's incident, but instead he challenged her accusers' judgment. In the midst of this exchange he wrote something in the dirt; no one knows what he may have been writing, although many have speculated. Maybe it was simply a distraction. He addressed the religious leaders and asked them a powerful question. He asked them to consider their own righteousness. Were they flawless? Of course not. The eldest left first; perhaps he had the wisdom to know how far he was from perfection and how unfit to be a judge. Everyone else eventually dropped their rocks as well. They lost their grounds for accusation in an encounter with Jesus, and they too were spared the impossible burden of acting as judge.

After dealing with the religious people, Jesus engaged with the woman herself, assuring her that the leaders had no grounds for condemning her and neither did he. Even though her actions were wrong, in her encounter with Jesus she was covered with mercy, grace, love, and a challenge to live differently. We can see that Jesus views the law through a lens of compassion. Oh, how great the love of Jesus is where mercy triumphs over judgment! We may never know if this loving encounter with Jesus changed her life, but we can hope that those who are forgiven much love much (Luke 7:47).

Personal Story

This story reminds me of an experience I had with a friend of mine, Joy. I met Joy while working in Kenya, where I spent six months living in a small village known for its sexual exploitation. My days were spent devoted to building relationships within the local community and caring for young girls at risk and in recovery from sexual trauma. My nights were spent praying for, visiting, and befriending women who were involved in prostitution and enslaved through human trafficking.

There was intense poverty in the town which caused many women to work the streets at night to provide for their children. Joy was one of the older women and had become a leader in her area. Every weekend I would find her near the same brothel, caught in a system that kept her from freedom. I shared many sodas with Joy and the other women while they shared their life stories with me. We talked about God, how much they hated what they had to do, and how they wanted different lives. They shared about the local churches not accepting them because they were known for being prostitutes and adulterers.

One night, as we were surrounded by harsh fluorescent lights, loud motorcycles, and louder music, I decided to quit trying to tell them about God and asked them if they had ever had a vision or a dream about Jesus. One by one, in a small circle, they said yes, over and over. Joy shared with intensity saying, "I was standing before this great man; it was Jesus. He was standing in front of a big book, a book that had names written of those who would be with him. I stood before him as he called out the names on the page. One by one, I waited for my name to be called, but he didn't read my name. I was so sad. I thought that my name wasn't there because of how I have been living my life on the streets. The man looked at me with compassion. He paused, as if for ten minutes, then strongly said to me, 'I'm not finished yet,' and turned the page. In a loud and loving voice he called my name, 'Joy Shama.' The first name he read was mine. I was so happy and relieved that I shouted out, 'Yes, Jesus!'"

It was as if time stopped there on that dusty street corner, and, in the midst of prostitution, drugs, alcohol, darkness, and hopelessness, my boxes of God's love were shattered. If I hoped that any good thing or "Christian-looking" life qualified me for a relationship with God, it was sucked away in that moment.

I saw Joy several more times before I got on a plane to return home. I continued to pray for her but didn't think I would ever know what happened with her life. That is, until pictures of her began showing on my Facebook newsfeed. Joy looked different. There was light in her eyes, she was dressed in beautiful traditional Kenyan clothing, and she was working . . . during the day. We became official friends on Facebook and began chatting. Joy updated me on her life, and I was so thankful to know that a few months after our team left, she left the streets. Joy explained her transformation: "It has been three years since I have worked the streets; others from your team helped me move into the house where you lived and start my own business. I am becoming a seamstress and running the chicken farm! My children are in school, and they are doing well. I am doing so well, and now I go to the streets at night to visit our friends who are still caught in the system. I buy them sodas and share God's love with them so they too can find a way to freedom, like me. I am training two girls to start their own businesses, and they are doing so well."

Tears of joy streamed down my face as I read her story and watched the power of God's love bring light into darkness. Like the woman caught in adultery, Joy was condemned by local religious leaders and thought she deserved to be cast out because of what she had done, but the deep love of God is still rewriting our endings so much better than we could ever imagine.

Joy experienced this reality and ended our talk saying, "Uncountable blessings. The Lord had mercy."

Jesus came to Joy in her darkest time and revealed to her that no matter what state she was in, in Christ nothing could separate her from God's love. Her name was written in that Book of Life. At some point, Joy opened her heart to Jesus. God didn't wait until she had her life all together because God's love didn't depend on her own put-togetherness. She had been desperate, caught in a system and looking for a way out, and it was there that God met her in her mess and loved her and then transformed her.

Maybe you've never been caught in adultery or faced the injustices of poverty that led you to do things you dreaded and felt condemned for, but maybe, like myself, you have never felt like anything you do is enough or something is always wrong with you, that you are unacceptable and unwanted because of your present or past experiences. Rest assured, God loves us and accepts us right where we are, and it is this kind of unconditional love that transforms us.

God invites us to come out of hiding, open our hearts, and receive this deep kind of love that seeps into every part of us, reminding us that we have worth, value, and purpose. I am confident that the Jesus who encountered the woman caught in adultery is the same Jesus who encountered Joy and is the same Jesus who meets us today, calling us by name and proclaiming over our own lives, "I'm not finished yet!"

Questions

1. What part of the story spoke to you the most? What is God saying to you? What is God asking you to do about it?

2. Consider a time in life when you thought there wouldn't be a second chance, but God extended grace to you. What was this like for you? How did this affect how you relate to others?

3. Where are you harshly judging yourself and others? Practice releasing judgment—it is not your job! Take a deep breath—you are accepted as you are.

Thought for Your Day

Sometimes our circumstances and choices put a period, an ending, in our lives, but in love, God puts a comma, turns the page, extends mercy, and invites us into a better ending than we could have ever dreamed.

Closing Prayer

God of love and infinite chances, thank you that in our worst and best moments your love remains constant. Thank you that you love us because love is who you are. Thank you for standing in the gap for us. When our lives are at risk of shame and we want to hide, cover us with your perfect love. Help us to experience your love and live free from the ways that once enslaved us. God, let your love in us pour out to love the one in front of us. Let this love saturate our communities and transform our world. All for you. Amen.

About the Author

Rev. Sophia Alexis Foutres holds a Master of Divinity from Palmer Theological Seminary of Eastern University and is an ordained minister at Cornerstone Christian Fellowship in West Chester, Pennsylvania. Sophia's work has been published in the *Clarion Journal of Spirituality and Justice*. She has served with Iris Global, an international ministry founded by Heidi and Rolland Baker, in several nations, where she saw God's love transform impossible situations. She has worked alongside those in recovery from drugs, alcohol, and trauma and currently serves as a hospice chaplain. Sophia is passionate to help people to know that they are deeply loved by God and experience the healing, wholeness, and freedom that comes from being connected to God, self, and others.

NOTE

1. Richard Rohr, https://www.goodreads.com/quotes/461968-most-of-us-were-taught-that-god-would-love-us, accessed November 2, 2018.

CONNECTING WITH YOUR STORY

2

The Canaanite Woman
Persistence in Faith

WADEEHA ANNE HENDERSON

But ask in faith, never doubting, for the one who doubts is like a wave of the sea, driven and tossed by the wind; for the doubter, being double-minded and unstable in every way, must not expect to receive anything from the Lord. —James 1:6-8

Hook Question

In the face of persistent adversities, do you remain steadfast in your faith, trusting God for deliverance, or do you succumb to the anguish of your tribulations?

Biblical Story: Matthew 15:21-28

Jesus left that place and went away to the district of Tyre and Sidon. Just then a Canaanite woman from that region came out and started shouting, "Have mercy on me, Lord, Son of David; my daughter is tormented by a demon." But he did not answer her at all. And his disciples came and urged him, saying, "Send her away, for she keeps shouting after us." He answered, "I was sent only to the lost sheep of the house of Israel." But she came and knelt before him, saying, "Lord, help me." He answered, "It is not fair to take the children's food and throw it to the dogs." She said, "Yes, Lord, yet even the dogs eat the crumbs that fall from their masters' table." Then Jesus answered her, "Woman, great is your faith! Let it be done for you as you wish." And her daughter was healed instantly.

Biblical Exposition

The story of the Canaanite woman in Matthew conveys the vital significance of having persistent faith. Throughout this narrative, the reader can comprehend that due to the faith of a Canaanite woman, Jesus made an exception to his earthly mission of being sent only to Israelites (known as the Hebrews or the Jews). This was the second and the last time that Jesus performed a miracle for a non-Jewish person in the Gospel of Matthew, with the first being for a centurion (Matthew 8:5-13). In both illustrations, it was the faith of the persons who pursued Jesus that caused him to extend his earthly assignment to include the Gentiles. These acts displayed by Jesus toward the Gentiles would be a foreshadowing of the ultimate universal kingdom mission presented later (see Matthew 24:14; 28:19)[1] of inclusivity for all of humanity.

Jesus left the place of Gennesaret (where the previous chapter last reported his place of reference) and entered an area known as Gentile territory, Tyre and Sidon.[2] When Jesus entered this region, a woman approached him looking for healing for her daughter. In Matthew, the woman is referred to as a Canaanite; whereas, in the biblical book of Mark, she is referred to as a Greek, "Syrophoenician" (see 7:24-30).[3] These two different terminologies are used interchangeably to convey this woman's non-Jewish heritage.

The Canaanite woman's daughter was afflicted by a demon and suffered greatly. Initially, Jesus was unresponsive toward the woman's request for healing. However, this did not deter her, as she continued to petition Jesus for a blessing. The disciples were irritated by the Canaanite woman's constant cries for help and beseeched Jesus to "send her away." It is at this point that Jesus stated to the woman that he was sent only to the people of Israel who were living in opposition to God. However, the Canaanite woman was not discouraged. In fact, she drew nearer to Jesus and humbled herself by kneeling before him as she continued to cry out for a blessing.

Jesus challenged the woman's plea for help and her action of humility when he made the quarrelsome statement that it was not just to take the children's food and give it to the dogs. The children referenced in this verse were God's chosen people of Israel, and the dogs represented the non-Jewish people, Gentiles. This comparison represented the preference of the children eating prior to feeding the dogs.[4] The food (NRSV) or bread (NIV) that is referred to in this verse is a representation "of the messianic fulfillment promised to and now in some way being made actual to Israel."[5] This emphasized God's faithfulness first to Israel, which is their "salvation-historical right (Romans 1:16)," prior to the mission being extended to the Gentiles (Matthew 24:14; 28:19).[6] Overall, it was the Canaanite woman's persistence in faith that enabled her daughter to be healed instantaneously.

Personal Story

Like many people, I have suffered much throughout my tenure of living on earth. But nothing could have prepared me for the devastation I was going to suffer in the spring of 2016. During this time, I suddenly became severely sick with several illnesses occurring simultaneously. Mental torment and excruciating physical pain accompanied me daily. The severity of the sickness was so great that I felt death lurking in my immediate future.

When I encountered the first symptoms of my illness, I was confused and unsettled about what was happening to me. However, I knew through personal experiences, biblical references, and theological studies that God is able to work abundantly, exceedingly beyond one's expectation. And so, I trusted wholeheartedly and had absolute faith in the Lord to work everything out for my good. With total faith in God for deliverance, I continued to pray as I continued to seek medical care. Within a matter of weeks, I had met with many types of doctors and specialists and had undergone multiple tests to find out what was plaguing my body.

As the months passed and my health deteriorated, my faith also declined. In an attempt to remain encouraged and steadfast in my faith, I decided to lean on what has always gotten me through tough times in the past: devotional practices such as prayers, fasting, and *lectio divina*, to name a few. But, at that point, nothing seemed to be helping. It appeared that the more severe my symptoms got, the more fear attacked my faith. I was unable to find the level of comfort, encouragement, hope, or peace that I longed for to deal with my medical situation.

During this period, I also had withdrawn and isolated myself from family and close friends and suffered in silence. After months of enduring daily pain, mental torment, and spiritual confusion, I began spiraling downward emotionally. I had finally reached a breaking point, one in which death occasionally seemed more appealing than living in constant torment. Throughout this time, my faith had been severely weakened, but I continued to cry out to the Lord for healing despite the persistent opposition of my declining health.

One day, after spiritual meditation, I realized that I was either going to trust in God's ability to work everything out for my good no matter the circumstances or continue to live in this horrific cycle between faith and fear. Since that day, I have decided to have absolute trust in God by canceling out fear moments with intentional self-talk that promotes persistent faith. For example, when moments of fear occur, I immediately combat those thoughts with an internal dialogue of trusting thoughts in the Lord in order to maintain strong faith. Although I have not been totally healed of all my afflictions yet, like the Canaanite woman, I will continuously pursue, plead, petition, and trust in God for healing no matter what the doctors or circumstances may convey.

Questions

1. How do you demonstrate persistence in your faith in the face of constant opposition?

2. What is your initial response when you encounter trials and tribulations in life?

3. Do the storms in your life bring you closer to God or do you seek refuge in secular things, vices, people, or your own abilities? Explain.

Thought for Your Day

Now faith is the substance of things hoped for,
the evidence of things not seen.
—Hebrews 11:1, KJV

Closing Prayer

Almighty and everlasting God, thank you for the daily blessings that you continuously bestow upon me. I come to the throne of grace asking that you increase my faith in areas in which I have unbelief or have yielded to fear. And, during moments of tribulations, I ask that you provide me with comfort, encouragement, and strength to remain steadfast and persistent in my faith. Amen.

About the Author

Wadeeha Anne Henderson is a student at Palmer Theological Seminary of Eastern University, where she is pursuing a Master of Divinity degree. She currently holds a Master of Science in Counseling Psychology and Human Services from Chestnut Hill College of Philadelphia, Pennsylvania. Wadeeha has served marginalized and disadvantaged communities as a psychotherapist, behavioral specialist, and mental health professional for the past eighteen years. Over the last five years, she has served as a board member of a non-profit organization, The Chapman Foundation, that provides reading and math tutoring services to economically disadvantaged inner-city youths.

NOTES

1. Donald A. Hagner, *Word Biblical Commentary*, vol. 33B (Dallas: Word, 1995), 443.

2. M. Eugene Boring, *The Gospel of Matthew*, vol. 8 of *The New Interpreter's Bible*, 87–505 (Nashville: Abingdon, 1995), 336.

3. David Hill, *The New Century Bible Commentary: The Gospel of Matthew* (Grand Rapids: Eerdmans, 1972), 253.

4. Hill, 254.

5. Hagner, 442.

6. Hagner, 443.

CONNECTING WITH YOUR STORY

3

The Widow of Zarephath

Less Is More

NATHANIEL JONES

*He is the reflection of God's glory and the exact
imprint of God's very being, and he sustains all
things by his powerful word.* —Hebrews 1:3a

Hook Question

Can you believe God will do a double miracle?

Biblical Story: 1 Kings 17:13-22

Elijah said to her, "Do not be afraid; go and do as you have
said; but first make me a little cake of it and bring it to me,
and afterwards make something for yourself and your son.
For thus says the LORD the God of Israel: The jar of meal will
not be emptied and the jug of oil will not fail until the day
that the LORD sends rain on the earth." She went and did as
Elijah said, so that she as well as he and her household ate
for many days. The jar of meal was not emptied, neither did
the jug of oil fail, according to the word of the LORD that he
spoke by Elijah.

After this the son of the woman, the mistress of the house, became ill; his illness was so severe that there was no breath left in him. She then said to Elijah, "What have you against me, O man of God? You have come to me to bring my sin to remembrance, and to cause the death of my son!" But he said to her, "Give me your son." He took him from her bosom, carried him up into the upper chamber where he was lodging, and laid him on his own bed. He cried out to the LORD, "O LORD my God, have you brought calamity even upon the widow with whom I am staying, by killing her son?" Then he stretched himself upon the child three times, and cried out to the LORD, "O LORD my God, let this child's life come into him again." The LORD listened to the voice of Elijah; the life of the child came into him again, and he revived.

Biblical Exposition

First Kings 17 begins with Elijah announcing to Ahab the word of the LORD: the land will endure a three-year drought (v. 1). After this, God commands Elijah to "hide" himself at the Wadi Cherith, where he is fed by ravens and drinks water from the brook. Lack of rain causes the Wadi to dry up, so Elijah is sent to a widow at Zarephath, who will feed him (1 Kings 17:8-9).

In the midst of a drought, a widow seems to be an unlikely source of help for Elijah. In ancient times, women were defined by their relationships with men and their dependence on them: from her father's household a woman would go to her husband's household; families desired sons, and sons were expected to care for a widowed mother. However, the son in this account is a child, dependent on his mother.

It is evident by reading the beginning of the text that the widow was either poor or frail from a lack of food considering that resources were scarce. Nonetheless, Elijah challenged her to make a cake of bread for him before making a cake for her and her son. He then prophesied to the widow that the jar of meal and jug of oil would not run dry until "the LORD sends rain" (1 Kings 17:14-16).

She followed all of Elijah's instructions, displaying obedience and faith. Later, when the widow's son died, she asked Elijah if he was convicting her of sin. Elijah questioned God if that was the reason for the child's death, but there was no apparent answer.[1] Rather, Elijah tried to restore the child's life, lying on the boy three times and pleading with God to restore his life. This was a life-giving symbol of the prophetic movement in ancient Israel, which involved using physical gestures to give a message. Elijah's lying on the boy was a way of telling his body to come to life. God answered Elijah's prayer by bringing the boy back to life. The widow was blessed by God with two miracles: the jar of meal and oil that would not run dry and the life of her son.

Personal Story

During my undergraduate years, I had a difficult experience with housing. I had signed up for a summer program that included free housing for the summer, but school policy for living on campus during the summer required me to work on campus. However, because I already owed a significant debt, the school would not allow me to work. About a month passed, and people began to doubt my chances of being allowed to remain in campus housing. I received criticism from my peers rather than encouragement. Throughout this entire time I prayed. Although God did not answer me right away, the school eventually allowed me to work on campus during the summer and used half of the money to pay my rent. My act of faith was to be still and follow God's leading, just as the widow of Zarephath had to have faith to feed Elijah before feeding herself and her son.

Years later I again found myself searching for housing. One night, I had a dream that I talked with a younger man and moved into a house. After this I found myself asking young people if they wanted to share housing. I did not find housing by talking to other young males around my age, but a young woman at the desk at my school referred me to a place called The Village, an off-campus apartment for students. It was there that I moved in with a younger man. When my own efforts seem to be met with dead ends, God made housing available. God spoke a word to me that I would get housing.

God can restore dead areas of your life, too. Elijah did not just perform a ritual, but he spoke to God in order to give life to the widow's son again. Both the widow's son and my dream are examples of how God will speak a word of restoration and life. Sometimes in life you are presented with two different challenges. This can be an opportunity for God to bless you twice. Both the challenges I encountered regarding housing were different, but God delivered me from both.

Sometimes God uses difficult circumstances to test your faith. God also proved to the widow that Elijah was a man of God. At the end of the text the woman stated her belief in Elijah as "a man of God" (1 Kings 17:24). The widow of Zarephath's test of faith pertaining to the oil and meal was a test of her obedience. She had to listen to what Elijah said. The test concerning her son's death was a test of her trust in God.

Questions

1. Have you ever struggled to believe a word from a preacher, pastor, or teacher? How did you respond to that word?

2. In the story of the widow, the miraculous and marginalization occur simultaneously. What experiences have you had, or has someone you know had, that are similar?

3. When have you witnessed God do more than one miracle in your life during the same time period? How did God work to meet your need?

Thought for Your Day

We may encounter difficulties in life, but sometimes God uses them as an opportunity to redeem us and reward our obedience.

Closing Prayer

Lord, I pray that you would help me to pass any tests of faith and to believe you to move on time in any area of life in which I am waiting for your answer. I pray that you would help me to trust you through any hardship and believe that you have purpose in it. Amen.

About the Author

Nathaniel Jones is a Master of Theology student from Palmer Seminary, a youth ministry worker, and an inspiring composer and musician with a Bachelor of Arts from Eastern University. His long-term goals are pastoring and composing gospel music.

NOTE

1. The text is ambiguous: Did the widow reference a specific sin that weighed on her, or in her grief did she blame herself for her son's death, supposing some general sin on her part was the reason for his death? Readers may be reminded of the question of Jesus' disciples: "'Rabbi, who sinned, this man or his parents, that he was born blind?' Jesus answered, 'Neither this man nor his parents sinned; he was born blind so that God's works might be revealed in him'" (John 9:2-3). It may be that the son's death and return to life, like the blindness of the man Jesus healed, occurred so that the works of God might be revealed in a time of widespread unbelief.

CONNECTING WITH YOUR STORY

4

Junia

Woman Apostle

DEBORAH SPINK WINTERS

The human race is a two-winged bird: one wing is female, the other is male. Unless both wings are equally developed the human race will not be able to fly. —Boutros Boutros-Ghali[1]

Hook Questions

In your lifetime, what jobs did you know where only men or only women could apply? Is it still that way today? Why?

Biblical Story: Romans 16:3-7

Greet Prisca and Aquila, who work with me in Christ Jesus, and who risked their necks for my life, to whom not only I give thanks, but also all the churches of the Gentiles. Greet also the church in their house. Greet my beloved Epaenetus, who was the first convert in Asia for Christ. Greet Mary, who has worked very hard among you. Greet Andronicus and Junia, my relatives who were in prison with me; they are prominent among the apostles, and they were in Christ before I was.

Biblical Exposition

One of the most controversial women of the Bible is someone you may have never heard of: Junia. In the biblical text she is mentioned only in the sixteenth chapter of Romans where Paul sends his greetings and recognizes those who have been instrumental in helping him and the early Christian church. In the society Paul was a part of, women rarely received honor from men, so the fact that Paul mentions women in his letter to the Romans is significant. That he specifically gives them honor for what they did is highly unusual for that time period.

Within this chapter, Paul highlights individuals as well as pairs of people and commends the work they have done. He highlights Prisca (also called Priscilla) and Aquila, a husband and wife team who are also mentioned in Acts 18:2, 1 Corinthians 16:19, and 2 Timothy 4:19. Paul also mentions Andronicus and Junia. Scholars know, due to the way their names are joined in the biblical text, that they are related in some way but are not sure if they are husband and wife, as Prisca and Aquilla were, or brother and sister. Paul adds that Andronicus and Junia were relatives of his who were also in prison with him and that they began to follow Christ before he did. And then Paul adds the most controversial statement of all, they were "prominent among the apostles." The very wording of the phrase implies that Andronicus and Junia were both apostles.

Throughout antiquity it had been accepted that Adronicus's partner in Romans 16:7 was a woman. It wasn't until medieval times that the question of whether Adronicus's partner was Junia, a female, or Junias, a male, began to be raised. Although there are many examples in Greek and Latin inscriptions of Junia representing a female name, there are no examples in Greek or Latin showing Junias as a male name or as the shortened form of the male name Junianus. This leads us to surmise it is simply because of the historical context where the leadership of women in the church began to be questioned that the example of a female apostle in the biblical text began to be questioned as well. It is rather amazing what context can do to our perceptions, something I was surprised to learn in my own ministry.

Personal Story

After I graduated from seminary, God called me to a small family-sized church (where I was the first solo female pastor in that community) with the mandate to grow both the size of the church and to grow people's perspectives of the idea of women in ministry. It has always amazed me how God manages to use us in ways we never expect.

I had been at my church for almost ten years when one of the very active families of our church told me they were going to miss the next Sunday because they were going to a baptismal service at another church. I appreciated them letting me know and thought nothing of it until the mother called me that next Sunday evening chuckling on the phone as she told me what had happened at the baptismal service.

As it turns out, the family had gone early to the church to make sure they could find it (this was before GPS and cell phones were used for directions like they are today) and so they could get a seat close enough that their young son would be able to see everything that took place. Since they were active members who were very involved in our Sunday school program and had various responsibilities during our worship service, it was rare that they visited other churches, so this was one of the few times their young son (who was just at the age that he was noticing things) was able to experience a different worship setting. They were enjoying pointing out what was different and similar between the church they were visiting and our church when the pastor stood up to begin the service.

The pastor was dressed in the normal robes of a more liturgical worship style, and as soon as he began to speak, the young son turned to his parents looking a little confused and asked them who the man speaking was. The mother whispered to her young son that he was the pastor of this church, at which point her young son's eyes grew big and in a very loud voice he exclaimed, "I DIDN'T KNOW MEN COULD BE PASTORS!"

I still chuckle at that today and the lessons it taught me about what and who I was teaching by simply being who God had called me to be and about how our perceptions of life are based on the context of what we are familiar with. For their young son, he just assumed because his pastor was a woman, only women could be pastors.

For me there is clear evidence in the biblical text that women were a natural part of the early church's leadership and that it probably wasn't until the church became institutionalized that women were moved to the background as men took on more of the leadership role. By medieval times the copyists of the biblical text were not familiar with women in leadership roles, and they began to question if it had ever been possible that women were leaders in the church. The name of Junia was maligned as a woman's name and changed to a man's name, for in their understanding it would be impossible to believe a woman could be an apostle. I wonder if Junia, who lived thousands of years ago, had any idea that she would be maligned and cause such a controversy in the Christian church just for being who God called her to be.

There is a responsibility that each of us has to be who God calls us to be. Sometimes it is a calling that fits the cultural norms of our day, but sometimes God calls us to help open minds that have become closed due to fears, sin, and evil. We are called in love to take a stand and God uses us to open doors and sometimes contexts that change the world.

Questions

1. Do you believe there are jobs that only men or only women should do? If so, what are they and why are they gender-specific?

2. What do you believe are women's and men's roles in the church today?

3. How in your life have you handled a situation where you were told you could not do something because of who you were? How would you handle it today?

Thought for Your Day

For we are God's handiwork,
created in Christ Jesus to do good works,
which God prepared in advance for us to do.
—Ephesians 2:10, NIV

Closing Prayer

Thank you, God, for who you created each of us to be. Help us to trust that you have given us exactly what we need to be able to accomplish the good works you have set before us. Give us the courage to believe, to trust, and to become exactly who we need to be for you. Amen.

About the Author

Rev. Dr. Deborah Spink Winters is an associate professor of Old Testament at Palmer Theological Seminary at Eastern University, on the faculty of www.coaching4clergy.com, co-founder of www.GodsPreciousChildren.com, founder of www.debwinterscoaching.com, and an ordained pastor in the United Church of Christ.

NOTE

1. https://www.slideshare.net/ecumenicalwomen/woman-power-point-doreen-boyd, slide #10, accessed November 2, 2018.

CONNECTING WITH YOUR STORY

5

Miriam

Generosity without Expected Reward

CASSIE PAULK HEINTZ

*Real generosity is doing something nice for some-
one who will never find out.* —Frank A. Clark[1]

Hook Questions

Are you able to give of yourself without expecting or desir-
ing reward and recognition? What is the reason you give of
yourself to others?

Biblical Story: Exodus 2:1-10

Now a man from the house of Levi went and married a Levite
woman. The woman conceived and bore a son; and when she
saw that he was a fine baby, she hid him three months. When
she could hide him no longer she got a papyrus basket for him,
and plastered it with bitumen and pitch; she put the child in
it and placed it among the reeds on the bank of the river. His
sister stood at a distance, to see what would happen to him.

The daughter of Pharaoh came down to bathe at the river, while her attendants walked beside the river. She saw the basket among the reeds and sent her maid to bring it. When she opened it, she saw the child. He was crying, and she took pity on him. "This must be one of the Hebrews' children," she said. Then his sister said to Pharaoh's daughter, "Shall I go and get you a nurse from the Hebrew women to nurse the child for you?" Pharaoh's daughter said to her, "Yes." So the girl went and called the child's mother. Pharaoh's daughter said to her, "Take this child and nurse it for me, and I will give you your wages." So the woman took the child and nursed it. When the child grew up, she brought him to Pharaoh's daughter, and she took him as her son. She named him Moses, "because," she said, "I drew him out of the water."

Biblical Exposition

In the chapter before this, Pharaoh made a decree which stated, "Every boy that is born to the Hebrews you shall throw into the Nile" (Exodus 1:22), which would include this new baby Moses. This decree was made because of Pharaoh's fear of the Israelites' rise in power in Egypt. This sets the stage for when we see Miriam following her baby brother in the basket along the Nile into the arms of Pharaoh's daughter.

At this point Miriam could only have been ten or twelve years old. The immense emotions she felt when Pharaoh's daughter found the baby must have been immeasurable. Without hesitation Miriam went to Pharaoh's daughter offering a solution to the need of a wet nurse. Miriam helped keep Moses alive through the offering of her mother as a wet nurse. In this era women were not generally seen as powerful or strong leaders and decision makers; however, in this moment young Miriam proved to be both, ensuring the future of her infant brother.

In the entirety of the Bible, Miriam never boasts of her quick thinking to save her brother. Her unconditional love and humility were evident in this story. Miriam used the gifts the Lord had given her to save the baby and shepherd him to safety into his true calling.

Personal Story

I was the middle child, not the oldest, not the baby. This comes with advantages, disadvantages, and "middle child syndrome," something which I definitely experienced, and to an extent still do. For the longest time, there were moments when I would not feel noticed, which was no fault of my parents. Because of this I tended to misbehave to get more attention, as I did not feel validated with what I was accomplishing in school or in my extracurricular activities.

When my dad married my stepmom, my family grew in size to seven, which enhanced any feeling of not being seen. There were now five children in my house, and, in my mind, four other people to compete for my parents' attention. Regardless of what was being done, I always had to be the center of attention.

Miriam, unlike me, seemed not to mind the lack of recognition and not being the center of attention. She displayed the miraculous ability to be humble, yet she used the gifts the Lord had given her when she offered a wet nurse to Pharaoh's daughter, essentially saving the baby's life. Never once, following this story, do you read of Miriam boasting or reminding others of her saving the life of Moses. Even in a moment that has the feel of sibling rivalry, when Miriam and Aaron argue with Moses over his Cushite wife and raise the question if God spoke only through Moses (Numbers 12), Miriam never goads Moses with, "Remember, I saved your life!"

It was not until I became more confident with myself and my abilities as a daughter, friend, employee, girlfriend, and child of God that I have been able to stop, be humble, and know that everything I do does not need to be noticed or recognized. There are moments when I regress to the "center of the universe Cassie," where I need the affirmation of my accomplishments from those around me. The gentle reminder of Miriam's actions throughout the years has been helpful to me. Throughout her life Miriam consistently served the Lord, using her gifts to lead, care for, and guide Moses, who in turn led the Israelites to freedom. I am learning to let the gifts which the Lord has given me shine through, not needing the recognition or approval of others for every one of my actions. I know my journey is far from over, and I am far from perfect, but I do know my willingness to become humble, to give of myself and my gifts without needing recognition.

Questions

1. What gifts do you have that enable you to serve others?

2. Think about yourself: what ways are you humble with your God-given gifts?

3. How can you be more like Miriam: powerful, smart, loving, praising the Lord through your humble, helpful presence?

Thought for Your Day

It is human nature to desire acceptance and recognition, but as Christians we are called to be like Miriam, to humbly use our God-given gifts to serve the Lord without seeking recognition.

Closing Prayer

Lord God, Creator of all, keep us humble, as Miriam was, mindful of our attention-seeking ways. Grant us humility as we allow our hearts, minds, and spirits to be content with the quiet giving of ourselves and our gifts as we serve you. Amen.

About the Author

Cassie Paulk Heintz grew up in the Presbyterian Church. Cassie has been and continues to be active in its various ministries. She is currently the administrative assistant to the executive presbyter of the Presbytery of Philadelphia and a full-time Master of Divinity Student at Palmer Theological Seminary. She and her husband, AJ, are expecting their first child.

NOTE

1. https://www.brainyquote.com/quotes/quotes/f/frankacla384551.html, accessed November 2, 2018.

CONNECTING WITH YOUR STORY

Part Two

Maligned Women

Maligned: misjudged, vilified, abused, and belittled based on the perceptions of others.

6

Hagar

The Strength to Persevere

PHYLLIS ALLENER MARTIN

And the angel of the Lord *said to her, . . . "the* Lord *has given heed to your affliction."*
—Genesis 16:11

Hook Question

Where are you coming from and where are you going?

Biblical Story: Genesis 16:1-10

Now Sarai, Abram's wife, bore him no children. She had an Egyptian slave-girl whose name was Hagar, and Sarai said to Abram, "You see that the Lord has prevented me from bearing children; go in to my slave-girl; it may be that I shall obtain children by her." And Abram listened to the voice of Sarai. So, after Abram had lived ten years in the land of Canaan, Sarai, Abram's wife, took Hagar the Egyptian, her slave-girl, and gave her to her husband Abram as a wife. He went in to Hagar, and she conceived; and when she saw that she had conceived, she looked with contempt on her mistress. Then

39

Sarai said to Abram, "May the wrong done to me be on you! I gave my slave-girl to your embrace, and when she saw that she had conceived, she looked on me with contempt. May the LORD judge between you and me!" But Abram said to Sarai, "Your slave-girl is in your power; do to her as you please." Then Sarai dealt harshly with her, and she ran away from her.

The angel of the Lord found her by a spring of water in the wilderness, the spring on the way to Shur. And he said, "Hagar, slave-girl of Sarai, where have you come from and where are you going?" She said, "I am running away from my mistress Sarai." The angel of the LORD said to her, "Return to your mistress, and submit to her." The angel of the LORD also said to her, "I will so greatly multiply your offspring that they cannot be counted for multitude."

Biblical Exposition

The saga of Abram, known as the father of faith; Sarai, his beautiful, postmenopausal, barren wife; and Hagar, the servant of his wife and the mother of his firstborn, is a fascinating story. The biblical story of Abram and his two wives, Sarai and Hagar, would be an interesting modern-day television promo even for twenty-first century readers—just scandalous. To Abram and Sarai, this barren couple, God made a covenant, a promise of a nation, a tremendous legacy of abundant children too many to count. Despite Sarai's postmenopausal reality, God promised this couple a biological miracle, their son Isaac.

Sarai devised a surrogacy plan that became the backdrop for Hagar's divine assignment. Sarai and her husband, Abram, became impatient waiting for God's promise of a child, which was delayed more than ten years. The impetuous Sarai wanted to experience motherhood and deferred gratification was no longer acceptable, so she helped actualize God's promise. Sarai gave her servant to her husband as a second wife to conceive, on her behalf, which satisfied her maternal instincts and social status as the bearer of an heir. Motherhood, the ability to produce an heir, was a matter of duty and honor. This practice of surrogacy, although difficult to accept in the twenty-first century, was an acceptable ancient custom, illustrated in Old Assyrian marriage contracts, the Code of Hammurabi, and the Nuzi tablets.[1] Sarai stopped looking for the miracle of God's promise and decided to replace it with a reality within her ability to produce.

Hagar was an Egyptian servant of Sarai who was not included in the Abrahamic covenant and was oblivious to the divine assignment from God that she would encounter. She became an unlikely suffering servant that God used to bless a nation. Once Hagar conceived, everything in the family's dynamics changed. Sarai and Hagar's reciprocal resentment became so profound that Hagar showed contempt for Sarai. After Hagar conceived the first heir to Abram's fortune, her attitude and status in that world's context changed. Sarai's jealousy became an unforeseen consequence of her procreation plan.

Whatever the reasoning for the change in these women's relationship, the result was disdain and disrespect. Sarai's plan had backfired. Her choice to circumvent God's plans for reproduction left her with the consequence of her self-imposed scheme. If only she knew what God revealed in Jeremiah 29:11, "For surely I know the plans I have for you, says the LORD, plans for your welfare and not for harm, to give you a future with hope." God chooses and uses the most unlikely persons as instruments to bless others.

Abram, now almost ninety, had an angry first wife whom he loved and a pregnant second wife who carried his first child, his only heir. He decided to allow Sarai to treat Hagar with unbearable cruelty, and Hagar responded by running away. Hagar, an Egyptian, a woman in a strange land a long way from home, chose to live in the wilderness unprotected, with no means of support, socially or economically, rather than to endure Sarai's cruelty. Her decision had suicidal characteristics, and yet it was the preferred destiny given Sarai's harsh treatment. Hagar had given up. How could she possibly survive on her own? I am so glad that there is an assurance in 1 Corinthians 10:13, "No testing has overtaken you that is not common to everyone. God is faithful, and he will not let you be tested beyond your strength, but with the testing he will also provide the way out so that you may be able to endure it."

This is the point in this Pentateuch text that it happened! Biblical history reveals a first! While in that wilderness experience, when Hagar was afraid and all alone, God sent a word of assurance to her. God blessed her and gave her a covenant promise similar to Abram's promise of many nations.

God asked Hagar, "Where did you come from and where are you going?" We see that Hagar was trying to go back to her homeland, Egypt, her past, but God sent her back to her future. Hagar was given an assignment to go back and give birth to the firstborn child of Abram, Ishmael. She was led back not to the safety of Egypt but to the cruelty of Sarai. The only difference between where Hagar came from and where she was returning was the covenant promise of God. Hagar would go back with the power of God to endure all obstacles. Hagar was not allowed to run away from her tragic dilemma. Instead, she was given the strength to persevere through the difficulties that awaited her. God gave Hagar the assurance that was part of the covenantal promise made to Abram; Ishmael would have so many descendants, she would not be able to count them all!

Personal Story

I entered seminary a healthy, fifty-year-old woman, filled with enthusiasm and cautiously apprehensive because of my age. I learned that God is not constricted with the concept of time or the season of my life. The call to ministry was one of the greatest things that had ever happened to me, and the path of seminary was necessary for my local church and our national convention, American Baptist Churches USA. But at the end of my first semester, I began to experience tremendous headaches that were progressive, intensifying and occurring with rapid frequency. After a month of headaches, I found myself in the hospital diagnosed with a brain cyst. This hospitalization was scary since the presence of the cyst compromised my ability to prepare for the great calling into the ministry. I cried to the Lord to remove the cyst on my brain through surgery, medication, or divine intervention. I convinced myself that I had the solution to my dilemma; the cyst had to be removed.

The doctors determined that neither surgery nor medication was needed and elected instead to monitor the size of the cyst. I returned to the class missing only one session. The problem was that my short-term memory was compromised. How could I return to school that summer and absorb the hundreds of pages in my books and journals with limited recall? Prior to this experience, I had a phenomenal memory. Now, the pace of seminary learning seemed insurmountable; however, I learned to reference Proverbs 3:5-6 as my daily mantra: "Trust in the LORD with all your heart, and do not rely on your own insight. In all your ways acknowledge him, and he will make straight your paths." My ability to complete this seminary journey eluded my natural comprehension. My family and friends tried to convince me to acquiesce to logic and terminate my seminary journey. I asked myself, "Where did you come from and where are you going?" Although I was frightened, a walk of faith was imperative, the only consideration since concession was not an option.

Similar to Hagar, I wanted to run away from the tremendous stress of a full-time job and full-time seminary classes. Full-time employment was essential because of my husband's unemployment through downsizing. Full-time seminary was imperative to maintain the 50 percent scholarship award. My limited retention was a daily reality. In those four years of seminary, I was diagnosed with a brain cyst, a heart aneurism, a major infection that required surgery and intravenous antibiotics, and a pulled ligament in the heart wall.

My only sister and best encourager was diagnosed with terminal cancer. For the first time in our lives, she had no support to offer during a life milestone. Again, like Hagar, I wanted to run into the wilderness and be finished with this assignment. Instead, I moved forward in my ministry calling with health concerns and without my best friend. I often felt lonely, incompetent, defeated, and unable to succeed. Not only was I struggling, but my support system was as well. I was conflicted between my family and ministry responsibility. I entered each semester by faith feeling skeptical and incomplete. I prayed and lamented to God, my only faithful refuge, and the Lord answered each cry.

I was not allowed to run away from those tragic dilemmas of health. Instead, I was given the strength to persevere through those difficulties that awaited me. I wanted the cyst and other health issues to go away. I needed a surrogate plan but learned that God's grace is sufficient (2 Corinthians 12:9). The Holy Spirit has taught me alternative ways to store the knowledge needed to navigate seminary, and in May 2015 I received a Masters of Divinity degree. God does not always move the mountains in our lives. God knows our past and our immediate wants and responds to our needs knowing our future.

Questions

1. Where did you come from in your ministry and where are you going?

2. When faced with a critical life dilemma, should retreat be a solution to consider? Explain your answer.

3. How do you navigate discrimination of age, race, creeds, gender, or national origin in ministry?

Thought for Your Day

In this journey of life God's blessings include those whom we might call "other." I am so glad since "other" includes me.

Closing Prayer

Dear Lord, thank you for the guidance of the Holy Spirit that leads us into the direction that brings hope to our lives. Thank you for seeing past our wants and providing for our needs. Lord, thank you for your protection in times that seem confusing; I know that you are working those difficult times out to blossom into blessings. Thank you, Lord, that you are a God who sees me! Amen.

About the Author

Rev. Phyllis Allener Martin serves as an ordained associate minister of the historic Kaighn Avenue Baptist Church in Camden, New Jersey. She holds a Master of Divinity from Palmer Theological Seminary at Eastern University, a Master of Social Work from Rutgers, the State University of New Jersey, and a Bachelor of Social Work from Saint Augustine College of North Carolina. She serves as adjunct chaplain for the hospital of the University of Pennsylvania. She and her husband of thirty-three years have three wonderful adult children.

NOTE

1. Martha T. Roth, *From the Ancient World: Law Collections from Mesopotamia and Asia Minor*, 2nd ed. (Atlanta: Scholars Press, 1997).

CONNECTING WITH YOUR STORY

7

The Ten Bridesmaids

Choose to Be the Person God Created You to Be

CAROLINE CORDA-RAZAT

It is our choices . . . that show what we truly are, far more than our abilities.
—J. K. Rowling, *The Chamber of Secrets*[1]

Hook Question

Your time and attention are precious to God. How could you spend them more wisely?

Biblical Story: Matthew 25:1-13

Then the kingdom of heaven will be like this. Ten bridesmaids took their lamps and went to meet the bridegroom. Five of them were foolish, and five were wise. When the foolish took their lamps, they took no oil with them; but the wise took flasks of oil with their lamps. As the bridegroom was delayed, all of them became drowsy and slept. But at midnight there was a shout, "Look! Here is the bridegroom! Come out to meet him." Then all those bridesmaids got up and trimmed their lamps. The foolish said to the wise, "Give us some of your oil, for our lamps are going out." But the wise replied, "No! There will not be enough for you and for us; you had better go to the dealers and buy some for yourselves." And while they went to buy it, the bridegroom came, and those who were ready went with him into the wedding banquet; and the door was shut. Later the other bridesmaids came also, saying, "Lord, lord, open to us." But he replied, "Truly I tell you, I do not know you." Keep awake therefore, for you know neither the day nor the hour.

Biblical Exposition

After desperately banging on the door hoping to be let in, the bridesmaids slumped down exhausted. Hands stinging and hearts still pounding from their frantic run, they hung their heads ashamed of having missed their opportunity. How could they have let this happen? But as I imagine this scene, I can't help but wonder if any bridesmaids felt maligned, bitterly grumbling about how selfish and stingy those inside had been by not sharing their oil.

At the time of Jesus, a wedding was a celebration for the entire community. Friends and neighbors would prepare with special clothes for the event, which could span days. Young women would have the joy and privilege of lighting the way for the wedding procession as they walked from celebrations at the home of the bride to the home of the groom. Here Jesus tells a parable about ten bridesmaids who had this responsibility with only half of them coming prepared and enjoying the reward. These wise women knew that sharing their oil would be risky. Indeed, if they divided the oil, all of the lamps could be lit for a short time, but they also might all run out before the night was through, leaving the entire procession in darkness. In the excitement and revelry, that was a tough but necessary decision to make. It is wise to stop and reflect on what is important and focus appropriately.

We can better understand the point of the parable of the ten bridesmaids when we notice that it sits among other stories in Matthew's Gospel that caution about keeping alert and being ready for a sudden but not unexpected arrival. These lessons lead up to the well-known passage in Matthew 25 about the separation of the sheep from the goats in which Jesus illustrates the distinction between two types of people: those who cared for others and will receive their inheritance and those who did not and will be shut out. Those who were rejected were not refused because of the bad they had done, but because of the good they had failed to do. This echoes the scene of the bridesmaids; although they *all* fell asleep while waiting for the bridegroom, it was only those who were unprepared to serve in the time of need who were left outside.

The ten woke with a start, yet the sudden shout was not the first indication that they should be ready. The bridesmaids knew well before they left home that they would need the oil. In fact, they had opportunities in the days prior to the event, days they spent dreaming about the wedding, choosing their wedding clothes, and hearing stories about the happenings at other weddings in the community—perhaps even some warning about foolish mistakes. Before we assume that the wise bridesmaids were being critical and mean, we need to be aware that there is no indication in the original text about the tone of the bridesmaids' conversation. It's possible that the prepared young women were frightened for their friends, pleading frantically that they run quickly, hoping that they would be able to return in time to join the festivities.

The foolish knew their responsibilities, and yet they chose not to focus on the most important requirement of the task, securing enough fuel for their lamps. To some it may seem they had been maligned by their friends. Although their mission might have seemed sudden, it in fact was not unexpected. They had to live with the consequences of their choice to be distracted from the work they were invited to do.

Personal Story

Let's hear it for the losers—the doubters, the tricksters, and the foolish. I can easily relate to many of them, and they have taught me much about my own humanity. Reading about the bridesmaids I am acutely aware of how, in the excitement of the celebrations, some of them could have been distracted, continually postponing the mundane task of getting a supply of oil. As they kept putting it off they surely thought, "Hey, it's simple; it won't take any time at all." There were so many people to talk to on that festive day, but there would surely be a moment for dropping into the shop to get provisions.

Those of us with adult attention deficit disorder can easily relate to the feeling of panic of not being prepared. Missing deadlines and forgetting details make me feel frustrated, angry, and ashamed. How can I be so educated and so foolish? I am creative and entertaining, and yet keeping my focus where it needs to be is a constant struggle. I tend to hyper-focus on what's interesting, not on what's relevant. To combat this, I have many strategies that work . . . when I remember to use them. I have special calendars and apps to keep me organized and on task. I limit my wardrobe, wearing mostly black or beige, and (shhhh) I have at least four pairs of the same ballerina flats, because when something works I have to stick with it. I have learned that when I keep my choices limited I can get dressed and out the door in the morning.

Many of us living with this type of brain have so many creative ideas that never make it out into the world because we spend all our energy on trying to make it through the day without being (too) late, feeling foolishly unprepared, or forgetting important details. I admit to my bad driving, chronic lateness, distractibility, and trouble with interrupting others. So if I interrupt you, don't miss my intention; it's not that I *lack* interest. It's that I am *too* interested and want to exchange stories. It's not really attention deficit; it's attention overload. People like me feel bombarded by information and therefore find it difficult to focus on one thing.

While writing this I'm thinking, "Girl, get over yourself, snap out of it, just do what needs to get done! People have real problems and you are complaining that you can't do what's in front of you—really?" (Hanging my head in shame.) "Really." "For goodness sake, take some medicine and move on." I am glad that many people can find relief that way, but I'm a bit jealous too, as I must work with other tools and strategies, solutions such as aerobic exercise, a low-sugar diet, and good sleep. Practicing mindfulness has been helpful, but it's not easy because my mind is full.

People without diagnosed attention deficit can also be lulled into distraction and fritter away their time. This is a struggle particularly for women who wear many hats and too often volunteer, willingly or not, to stand in the gap to help others. Guarding our time and energy and using them wisely is an important skill to learn. We must take care to focus on the interesting *and* important things in life. We must not be afraid to be like the wise bridesmaids, discerning what is important and making time for it.

God has created each of us to be a beautiful package—a unique intersection of personality, abilities, interests, imperfections, experiences, specific opportunities, and holy discontent. We are individually equipped to reflect the light and love of Jesus into the world around us, and we must honor that call. The bridesmaids had been chosen for a mission. Those who kept their focus on what was important had the joy of lighting the way for others and participating in the celebration with the bridegroom. Those who frittered away their time found themselves in the dark, exhausted from banging on the door, begging to be let into the banquet.

I used to think that God had time only for the big things in life, the dramatic and the tragic. But I've learned that God is big enough to be present even in my daily struggle with my attention and energy. When I am mindful about where I am putting my focus, God is able to call me out on any time wasting.

Daily time in the Word has become an essential discipline for me. Listening to audio readings has made this habit easier. Reflecting on Bible stories and situations gives me the space to think about my priorities, and dedicating that time each morning has substantially improved my focus. Here the bridesmaids remind me that we are each uniquely chosen vessels to shine Jesus' love and light; in response, I choose to honor my role and not allow distractions to jeopardize the opportunities I have been given. Small choices can change the direction of a life.

I use many strategies to manage my attention deficit, and when I invite God into those strategies the results are remarkable. I know I will falter, but it's okay as long as I stick to my plan, taking it one day at a time, trusting that God is with me as I prepare my extra oil, ready to serve when the need arises.

Questions

1. The bridesmaids might have dreamed of having the privilege and thrill of dressing up and carrying a lamp for a bride from the time they were little girls. Spend a few minutes dreaming about your future self. What thrilling way are you able to serve others?

2. How could you begin to prepare for that dream vocation? (For example: You might reflect on past dreams, talk with friends about how they perceive your gifts, and spend time in silent prayer, asking the Spirit to speak.)

3. In what situations do you feel distracted? How can you check in with yourself so that you don't lose focus on what is important for your day, week, month, or year?

Thought for Your Day

Be who God meant you to be
and you will set the world on fire.
—Catherine of Siena[2]

Closing Prayer

Lord, I praise you that you are the sovereign Creator of the universe and you love me. Thank you for forming me as a unique vessel created to shine your light into the world and that my time and attention are precious to you. Thank you for the unique intersection of my personality, gifts, interests, imperfections, experiences, opportunities, and holy discontent. Lord, please show me how I might continue to become the person you have created me to be. Gently make me aware when I am living in my calling and when I am being distracted from it. As I go about my daily responsibilities please guide me in my choices for my time and attention that they may honor you and your creation. Amen.

About the Author

Caroline Corda-Razat has an MBA from New York University and an MDiv from Palmer Theological Seminary. She has worked with women from across the globe as a retreat speaker and teacher. Caroline uses her unique brand of humor and energy to encourage and equip people for deepening their faith and transforming their world. Her latest project includes research on how the church can better understand and energize women in the critical flexion point of midlife. When she is not in Pennsylvania, she might be back at her dream job sharing the Good News in Paris as a docent at Notre Dame Cathedral. For a list of her personal ADHD strategies go to CarolineRazat.com.

NOTES

1. https://www.goodreads.com/quotes/12415-it-is-our-choices-harry-that-show-what-we-truly, accessed November 2, 2018.

2. https://www.goodreads.com/quotes/20893-be-who-god-meant-you-to-be-and-you-will, accessed November 2, 2018.

CONNECTING WITH YOUR STORY

8
Lot's Wife
Leave Your Past in the Past

SARAH WALLACE WATERS

*You can't look back—you just have to put the
past behind you and find something better in your
future.* —Jodi Picoult, *Salem Falls*[1]

Hook Question

Are you doomed to repeat your past?

Biblical Story: Genesis 19:15-26

When morning dawned, the angels urged Lot, saying, "Get
up, take your wife and your two daughters who are here, or
else you will be consumed in the punishment of the city." But
he lingered; so the men seized him and his wife and his two
daughters by the hand, the LORD being merciful to him, and
they brought him out and left him outside the city. When they
had brought them outside, they said, "Flee for your life; do
not look back or stop anywhere in the Plain; flee to the hills,
or else you will be consumed." And Lot said to them, "Oh,
no, my lords; your servant has found favor with you, and you

55

have shown me great kindness in saving my life; but I cannot flee to the hills, for fear the disaster will overtake me and I die. Look, that city is near enough to flee to, and it is a little one. Let me escape there—is it not a little one? —and my life will be saved!" He said to him, "Very well, I grant you this favor too, and will not overthrow the city of which you have spoken. Hurry, escape there, for I can do nothing until you arrive there." Therefore the city was called Zoar. The sun had risen on the earth when Lot came to Zoar.

Then the LORD rained on Sodom and Gomorrah sulfur and fire from the LORD out of heaven; and he overthrew those cities, and all the Plain, and all the inhabitants of the cities, and what grew on the ground. But Lot's wife, behind him, looked back, and she became a pillar of salt.

Biblical Exposition

At the beginning of Genesis 19, Lot invited the two angels into his home. He provided them with a big feast, and after Lot and his guests had eaten, the men of Sodom surrounded Lot's house. They wanted to force the strangers outside and have sex with them. However, Lot knew the two men were angels and wanted to protect them. Instead he offered his two daughters to the men of Sodom.

You may wonder where Lot's wife was. Why did she not stand up against Lot, and why did she not try to protect her daughters? Throughout the text, Lot's wife is unnamed. She is not mentioned or seen as important in protecting her family; she remained silent. But she must have been there.

Likewise, when Lot and his family were urged to flee Sodom, she remained silent. The angels told them, "Flee for your life; do not look back or stop." Readers may wonder if Lot told his wife and daughters the command. Yet, Lot's wife looked back and became a pillar of salt. Did she long for her past? Did she fear what was waiting for her in the future? God wanted to save her along with her family. She had only to follow God's command, but her disobedience led to her death. Her actions at the end of the text hold a reminder: when God commands us to go forward, do not question. Luke 17:32 tells us to remember Lot's wife. God wants us to understand that God means what God says.

Personal Story

As a child, I was raised within the church. My mother worked as the director of religious education for the Archdiocese of Philadelphia. I followed the commands of my mother and attended church every Sunday. However, I loved the fast life and would run with the wrong crowd every chance I could get. I spent my teenage years around drug dealers, promiscuous teens, and car thieves. As a young adult I dropped out of college and began to have children. I struggled and did anything and everything to survive. I used men to get what I wanted and needed. I would have them believing they were number one in my life but only manipulated them for money. I was known as the biggest female player in my neighborhood.

What is a player? A player is a person who uses or plays with people's emotions without caring about the outcome. You need to get whatever you can from them without allowing yourself to fall in love or get played by them.

At times things got so bad that I began to use other women to earn a profit. I would pimp them out to men, and I never cared about the danger for them or me. I just wanted to continue to make quick money, and pimping was the way to get it. You see, I was living in a town like Sodom, and I became content. I never allowed myself to feel shame for my actions until I began to witness how my actions were affecting my relationship with my family. I loved money and what it could buy; however, I did not love the perception others had of me. I remember wanting and waiting for God to save me. Was God listening? Did God care? I began to believe God was punishing me for my actions.

However, I still did not feel important or wanted enough for God to save me. I too was Lot's wife: present, unwanted, not important enough to make the right choices. I was in love with the things of my past, but my soul cried out. I prayed for God to save me. However, I was not willing to leave my past. When God pushed me to move forward, I too looked back with longing and mourned my past. Was I doomed to repeat my past? Yes, and I was ready to repeat it, or so I thought. You see, as I began to repeat my past, I lost everything. My job, home, money, and family were gone. God was still there waiting for me to cry out for help, waiting for me to listen to God's command. But like Lot's wife I feared my future.

I was so caught up in my past that I was blocking my blessings. God heard my cries. God was moving me forward, but I did not trust the outcome. I heard the command but refused to believe God was speaking to me. I was no longer in the church, I was no longer a Christian, and I was no longer a child of God. However, God's command was for me and only me. I was this woman who left the church and began practicing Islam. God reached down and whispered in my ear, "Move." As I am telling you this, I realized that one command was not a punishment but a lifesaver. God provides us with the chance to run to safety, but we take that last glance of our past and punish ourselves. The story of Lot's wife taught me to follow God's command. God's reward for you is better than your own punishment.

Questions

1. How have you blocked your blessings?

2. How have you followed God's command?

3. In what ways do you identify with Lot's wife? How are you similar and how are you different?

Thought for Your Day

God calls us to move forward and not look back. We have to be willing to leave our past for God, for taking that last glance into our past will hinder our future.

Closing Prayer

Heavenly Father, I cry out to you with tears from my past. I cry out to you with tears for my future. Continue to move and push me to go forward without hesitating. I know you have me covered with your blood and I am protected by your grace and mercy. I will follow your command, for you know me best. I am saved by your unconditional love for me. Amen.

About the Author

Sarah Wallace Waters is a student in the Master of Theological Studies program at Palmer Seminary. She is the evangelist leader and adult Sunday school teacher at Holy Trinity Baptist Church. In June 2018, Sarah became the first licensed female minister of Holy Trinity Baptist Church. Her long-term goals are ministering and spreading the Word of God through Christian counseling. It is her hope to help others push through their storms of life as God has enabled her to push through her own.

NOTE

1. https://www.goodreads.com/work/quotes/3349637-salem-falls, accessed November 2, 2018.

CONNECTING WITH YOUR STORY

9

Jael

Pegged All Wrong

TASEY BURTON

*And she said, "I will surely go with you;
nevertheless, the road on which you are going will
not lead to your glory, for the LORD will sell Sisera
into the hand of a woman."* —Judges 4:9

Hook Question

When have you allowed God to use you in a way that you or
others never thought possible?

Biblical Story: Judges 4:17-22

Now Sisera had fled away on foot to the tent of Jael wife of
Heber the Kenite; for there was peace between King Jabin
of Hazor and the clan of Heber the Kenite. Jael came out
to meet Sisera, and said to him, "Turn aside, my lord, turn
aside to me; have no fear." So he turned aside to her into the
tent, and she covered him with a rug. Then he said to her,
"Please give me a little water to drink; for I am thirsty." So
she opened a skin of milk and gave him a drink and covered

him. He said to her, "Stand at the entrance of the tent, and if anybody comes and asks you, 'Is anyone here?' say, 'No.'" But Jael wife of Heber took a tent peg, and took a hammer in her hand, and went softly to him and drove the peg into his temple, until it went down into the ground—he was lying fast asleep from weariness—and he died. Then, as Barak came in pursuit of Sisera, Jael went out to meet him, and said to him, "Come, and I will show you the man whom you are seeking." So he went into her tent; and there was Sisera lying dead, with the tent peg in his temple.

Biblical Exposition

The book of Judges is the account of Israel's history from the death of Joshua to the monarchy. Over this span of time, Judges deals with Israel's actions under the leadership of thirteen judges and illustrates the circular pattern of sin, repentance, and restoration in its relationship with God. Israel was often guilty of the sin of idolatry, which brought about oppression and domination by other nations. Under the leadership of Deborah, the fourth judge, Israel was delivered from its oppressor in the most unexpected way. She called forth Barak, who was commanded by God to go up against Sisera with ten thousand men from the tribes of Naphtali and Zebulun, but he refused to go without her. She prophesied that since he refused to go without her, Sisera would be given into the hands of a woman. As instructed by God, they went into battle and the Lord caused them to be victorious. All of the men in Jabin's army were killed except for Sisera, who abandoned his chariot and fled on foot. He went to the tent of Jael, wife of Heber the Kenite. Sisera assumed that he would find safety there because the Kenites were at peace with King Jabin. His choice made it obvious that he did not see Jael as a threat; somehow he eluded capture by Barak, who was in pursuit of him. Sisera could not have been more wrong in his assumption.

When we are introduced to Jael we find her alone in her tent. It is very likely that she was attending to the everyday upkeep of her home and needs of her family. It probably never occurred to her that God would interrupt the pattern of her daily routine to accomplish God's plan for Israel. Not far from her home there was a war raging between Israel and King Jabin's army. Sisera, the commander of King Jabin's army, had nine hundred iron chariots at his disposal, and he had been a cruel oppressor of the Israelites for twenty years. God gave the Israelites over to their enemies because of their idolatrous practices, and, as a result, Jabin's reign of terror had gotten so bad that the land was desolate, people were afraid to travel, the fields had not been tended, and Israel felt defenseless against the army's iron chariots.

No one will ever know what Jael was thinking when she came out to meet Sisera and invited him into the tent. Did she know how drastically her life would change in that encounter? Did she even see this coming? There is no mention of her knowing about the prophecy given by Deborah, and even so, Deborah never *named* the woman. Some say Jael's act was cruel and premeditated, while others believe it was the fulfillment of prophecy; God did indeed give Sisera into the hands of a woman! God used a woman skilled at erecting tents to bring down a man who had terrorized Israel for two decades. Where Sisera's iron chariots failed to save him, a woman with a tent peg and a hammer annihilated a long-time oppressor of Israel. Jael allowed herself to be used by God to accomplish God's will concerning Israel.

Personal Story

I must admit, I *never* saw it coming. It never occurred to me that God would change my life in such a way. I distinctly remember sitting quietly praying for my husband while he was being examined by the ordination council for the pastorate. I sensed that God had been preparing him for years to serve as a pastor; I could see the transformation taking place, and I was supportive when he accepted his call. This path was new to both of us, so I was a bit nervous about this council of pastors who had gathered to "examine" my husband. Rather than pace or fidget I chose to intercede quietly for my husband.

As I prayed, I heard God say that it was not *just* my husband that God had chosen, but it was me as well. I shifted in my seat, sure that I had somehow misunderstood. I was a busy wife and mother with three young children under the age of ten. I loved God and was intentional about growing in my faith and relationship with God. Both my husband and I were active in our church; he had been leading a men's ministry for six years, and I had been leading a women's ministry for about three years. I was content. Life was good.

I continued to pray, and as I sat there, I thought about how I could assist my husband in his new role as a pastor. I could type his sermons and get his office set up and organized because I had the gift of administration; that would be a great help to him. In the silence of the room, I heard God again. God did not want me to be my husband's secretary or administrator. It was clear to me that serving alongside my husband as an ordained minister in my own right was what God wanted. To serve as a secretary would not absolve me of God's intended purpose for my life as a pastor. Any response less than "Yes, Lord" would have been an act of disobedience.

I squirmed in my seat. "*Me*, God? The *me* that you and I both know? I don't like speaking in front of people. I don't know any female pastors personally. No female in my family has ever been a pastor! I don't know how to be a pastor. Are you sure, God?" The intensity of the message God conveyed did not lessen with my questions; the seriousness of the message remained. I wanted to honor God through my obedience, but I did not want to do this. I had spent my childhood and young adult years in a denomination where it was extremely rare to have female pastors. I never aspired to this. I was already struggling to meet the demands as a wife and mother; there already weren't enough hours in the day!

Despite my objections, it was more important to me to honor God with obedience. I accepted the call to pastor. "Okay, God, since *you* want this, *you* have to help me, show me how!" God had interrupted my plans and goals with a plan of God's own. God did help me, with every challenge and every growing edge.

The reality is that God called me and I answered the call, and it does not matter how unexpected it was. My inability to anticipate God's call did not render me unable, ineffective, or unacceptable to pastor. God has indeed called women to serve as pastors; gender is not a hindrance to God.

As was the case with Jael, the Lord presented me with an unexpected call. The text doesn't say whether Jael wondered about her call, as I did initially, but she was obedient. And as I pondered God's call, it became clear that I too was called to obedience, to serve and encourage the people of God.

Questions

1. What has God called you to do that you didn't see coming?

2. What role has your gender played in your response to God's call?

3. What opposition have you experienced? How have you responded?

Thought for Your Day

Embrace God's plan for your life. It will help you to avoid unnecessary struggles.

Closing Prayer

God, we thank you that your plans for us are intentional and strategic. Before you formed us, you knew us, and it does not matter to you how we differ from others; you created us with purpose. Help us to embrace the plans you have for our lives. Let us not be deterred by our perceived flaws and shortcomings or even the opinions or theology of others. Rather, help us to graciously serve others in love for your honor and glory. We trust your faithfulness and know that you will always do what is best for us. In Jesus' name we pray. Amen.

About the Author

Tasey Burton is copastor and cofounder of Perfect Will Ministries in New Castle, Delaware. She has served in this capacity with her husband, Frank, for the past fifteen years. She completed her Master of Divinity at Palmer Theological Seminary in May 2017. She is also founder of Under the Shadow of the Almighty Women's Ministry, a ministry that helps women grow in faith and not lose themselves in the many roles they have as they navigate through life.

Jael

CONNECTING WITH YOUR STORY

10

Jezebel

Manipulator or Manipulated?

DEBORAH SPINK WINTERS

*The people who would like to manipulate and use
you won't tell you your blind spots. They may
plan to continue using them to their advantage.*
—Assegid Habtewold, *The 9 Cardinal Building
Blocks: For Continued Success in Leadership*[1]

Hook Question

Are you ever justified in knowingly manipulating someone?

Biblical Story: 1 Kings 21:1-7

Later the following events took place: Naboth the Jezreelite
had a vineyard in Jezreel, beside the palace of King Ahab of
Samaria. And Ahab said to Naboth, "Give me your vineyard,
so that I may have it for a vegetable garden, because it is
near my house; I will give you a better vineyard for it; or, if
it seems good to you, I will give you its value in money." But
Naboth said to Ahab, "The LORD forbid that I should give
you my ancestral inheritance." Ahab went home resentful

and sullen because of what Naboth the Jezreelite had said to him; for he had said, "I will not give you my ancestral inheritance." He lay down on his bed, turned away his face, and would not eat.

His wife Jezebel came to him and said, "Why are you so depressed that you will not eat?" He said to her, "Because I spoke to Naboth the Jezreelite and said to him, 'Give me your vineyard for money; or else, if you prefer, I will give you another vineyard for it'; but he answered, 'I will not give you my vineyard.'" His wife Jezebel said to him, "Do you now govern Israel? Get up, eat some food, and be cheerful; I will give you the vineyard of Naboth the Jezreelite."

Biblical Exposition

Every year when I teach my Historical Books class at Palmer Theological Seminary at Eastern University, I ask my class if they know anyone named Jezebel in today's world. Over the past seventeen years, I have had three students raise their hands, two of whom were students from another country. It speaks to how powerfully the reputation of Jezebel still holds influence, as very few people want to name their daughters Jezebel.

It is not uncommon even today to hear someone call a woman who is promiscuous "you Jezebel, you!" It is believed Jezebel's reputation of a promiscuous woman comes from the way she met her death. Much like a general will dress himself in full regalia as he prepares for war, so Jezebel, when facing what turned out to be her final battle, painted her eyes and adorned her head trying to muster supporters to her cause. It did not work, as she was thrown from the very window she had called for help from, and the wild dogs ate all but her skull, her feet, and the palms of her hands. The fact that she painted her face and put on her finery to try and lure people to her has led some to make the association with Jezebel and other "painted ladies" of that day—prostitutes!

There is no question in the biblical text that Jezebel learned to be a very strong woman. She is the daughter of King Ethbaal of Sidon. She is probably given in marriage to King Ahab of Israel to keep peace between those two nations. It is just a matter of time before we see her influence on her husband, Ahab, as she instituted the worship of Baal and Asherah instead of Yahweh and went so far as to try and kill all the prophets of Yahweh including Elijah, one of Yahweh's greatest prophets.

There is part of me that wonders if Jezebel's reputation and actions are totally her fault, particularly in the story of Naboth. It is King Ahab who wants Naboth's field, and when he cannot get it, he appears to take to his bed in a pouting fit like a spoiled child. Does Naboth do this because he feels there is no hope of attaining Naboth's field, or does he do it on purpose knowing that all he need do is play the pouting child so that his wife will do the dirty work for him? Jezebel does do her husband's dirty work, and it is not long before Naboth is killed and Ahab owns his field.

As the saying goes in our culture, "It takes one to know one." My brother and sisters will tell you I was a master manipulator growing up. As I read this text, I wonder if Ahab knew exactly what he was doing. There is no question Jezebel did some horrible things when she was queen, but did she act alone in all of it, or was she a pawn of her husband, Ahab?

Personal Story

I am very proud of the fact that I grew up a PK (pastor's kid), and as I have studied pastors' kids I have come to believe that we fit into three categories. The one that is best known is the pastor's kid who rebels against everything his or her parent, the pastor, stands for. There are various ways to do this, and, as you consider all the various pastors' children you have known, I am guessing you could easily name one or two who were the typical "hell-raiser" instead of "kin-dom-builder" children you would expect a pastor to be raising.

The second type is what I call the "angel." This pastor's kid tries to live up to all of the expectations everyone in the congregation puts on them since they are the "pastor's kid," after all. I have found this type can pull it off for a while, but eventually, and often when they get older, they have to come to terms with who everyone else tells them they should be and who it is God has created and called them to be. For some this can be a very long road. Maybe you know some of these pastors' kids as well?

And then there is my type. We are the ones who learn how to look angelic but get exactly what we want out of the system by manipulating the heck out of it with usually no one being the wiser. Jesus tells the parable of the father who goes to his two sons and asks the one to do some work for him. The son says, "No way" but later repents and does it. And then the other son says, "Sure, Dad, I'll do it" but never does. I always figured for some reason Jesus left out my approach: "Sure Dad, I'll do it" and then manipulate someone else to go do it for me! I look great and the job gets done; who cares about the person I manipulated!

It took God working a long time in my life for me to come to the realization that as much as I did not like it when I realized I had been manipulated, others didn't like it when they realized I had manipulated them. As I reflect on Jezebel's story I wonder if she became exasperated with Ahab's childish tantrums as he took to his bed one more time when he didn't get his way. She may have thought it was far easier for her to fix the situation for her husband than to deal with his moaning and groaning and allow him to deal with the consequences of his own actions or, in this case, lack of action. That's exactly what a master manipulator would want you to feel—like your actions are making it easier on you and then you end up doing your manipulator's work while they barely lift a finger.

I don't emulate Jezebel, but I do believe she may have fallen into a trap that can happen in any relationship, whether it is between spouses, siblings, friends, colleagues, bosses and employees, etc. In every relationship we have the choice to manipulate the other person, as Ahab may well have been doing with Jezebel to get her to do his dirty work, or to be manipulated.

As for me, I am a recovering manipulator. I seek God's guidance in the relationships in my life and strive to be authentic in my actions and non-actions, and I am learning to live with the consequences. I also strive *not* to "fix" other people, particularly my students but, where able, help them realize the consequences of their own actions or inactions so they can make healthier choices in their lives.

It is not always easy, but I am learning to be there to support and help other people as we partner together in life without manipulating them to be who I want them to be. It is a much more fascinating and exciting journey to watch people begin to take responsibility for their lives and who God is calling them to be. I wonder who Jezebel could have been had she not been manipulated or been a manipulator! Just think how different her story would have been!

Questions

1. When have you witnessed a relationship based on manipulation, whether your own or someone else's? What were the signs?

2. What do you do when you realize a relationship is based on manipulation? What steps can you take to make it a healthier relationship?

3. When has someone tried to manipulate you? How did you react? When have you tried to manipulate someone else? What happened?

Thought for Your Day

Love comes when manipulation stops;
when you think more about the other person
than about his or her reactions to you.
When you dare to reveal yourself fully.
When you dare to be vulnerable.
—Joyce Brothers[2]

Closing Prayer

Creator of the universe, forgive us when we try to control other people's lives, when we start to manipulate others because we think we know what is best for them as well as ourselves. Help us be vulnerable and trust you to help us be who you have called us to be regardless of what others think or say about us. Help us to let others be their true selves as they follow you. Help us to love. Amen.

About the Author

Rev. Dr. Deborah Spink Winters is associate professor of Old Testament at Palmer Theological Seminary at Eastern University, on the faculty of www. coaching4clergy.com, co-founder of www.GodsPreciousChildren.com, a professional certified coach with the International Coaching Foundation and Center for Progressive Renewal, founder of www.debwinterscoaching. com, and an ordained pastor in the United Church of Christ.

NOTES

1. http://www.goodreads.com/work/quotes/40192152-the-9-cardinal-building-blocks-for-continued-success-in-leadership, accessed November 2, 2018.

2. https://www.brainyquote.com/quotes/quotes/j/joycebroth143030.html, accessed November 2, 2018.

CONNECTING WITH YOUR STORY

Part Three

Miraculous Women

Miraculous: having overcome great odds by divine encounter or through divine enablement.

11

Daughters of Zelophehad
They Tried It!

DANNITA L. BROOKER

I can accept failure, everyone fails at something.
But I can't accept not trying. —Michael Jordan[1]

Hook Question

Will you stand up for what is right?

Biblical Story: Numbers 27:1-8

Then the daughters of Zelophehad came forward. Zelophehad was son of Hepher son of Gilead son of Makir son of Manasseh son of Joseph. The names of the daughters were: Mahlah, Noah, Hoglah, Milcah, and Tirzah. They stood before Moses, Eleazar the priest, the leaders, and all the congregation, at the entrance of the tent of meeting, and they said, "Our father died in the wilderness; he was not among the company of those who gathered themselves together against the LORD in the company of Korah, but died for his own sin; and he had no sons. Why should the name of our father be taken away from his clan because he had no son? Give to us a possession among our father's brothers."

Moses brought their case before the LORD. And the LORD spoke to Moses, saying: "The daughters of Zelophehad are right in what they are saying; you shall indeed let them possess an inheritance among their father's brothers and pass the inheritance of their father on to them. You shall also say to the Israelites, 'If a man dies, and has no son, then you shall pass his inheritance on to his daughter.'"

Bible Exposition

Numbers 27:1-8 tells the fascinating story of the five daughters of Zelophehad. Zelophehad died during the forty years when the Israelites were wandering in the wilderness. During the time in the wilderness there was a rebellion against Moses orchestrated by Korah. The daughters challenged the judicial system regarding the question of female inheritance. The five daughters approached Moses and the elders, as well as God, with a claim about the ownership of land. The law was very clear during this time regarding land ownership. Deuteronomy 21:15-17 said that property is passed on only to male heirs. Also, the oldest son received a double portion. No widow or daughters would receive any portions of the estate, but their male relatives were obligated to care for them.

The daughters solidified their argument by including the declaration that their father had not been involved in the insurrection of Korah and his associates against the authority of Moses and Aaron. Utilizing this approach, the daughters made the court aware that they could not use the argument of participating in the rebellion as just cause to prevent the transfer of Zelophehad's property to his lawful heirs, and it was this legal status that they claimed.

The daughters argued that since there was no male heir, their father's name or lineage should not be cut off from his family. They did not want their father's name to be forgotten, and to avoid this injustice, the daughters should be permitted to inherit his estate. Moses consulted God, and God affirmed that the five sisters had a just cause; their plea compelled God to change the law regarding female inheritance.

Can we imagine the fear these women must have felt as they confronted Moses with this unusual request? The sisters had no models for this kind of confrontation coming from women, but they did it anyway. Unity can yield courage and strength.

The daughters' courageous action emerged as a symbol of the powerless standing up for what is right. This story serves as an example that laws can be challenged and changed by the authorities, both human and divine, in recognition of the needs of the disenfranchised. We must learn how to give ourselves the license to change traditions. The sisters challenged power, achieved a measure of justice, and learned something of what those engaged in struggle experience all too often: "two steps forward, one step back," but we keep on pushing. They tried it!

Personal Story

I grew up during the Civil Rights era. As a child, I remember hearing my parents talk about the indignities that African Americans suffered due to segregation and discrimination. My parents participated in the demonstrations, and I recall being with my mother and grandmother as a young child to hear Rev. Dr. Martin Luther King Jr. He made a great impression on me as a child, as did Rosa Parks, who refused to give up her seat on a public bus to make room for a white passenger. She was arrested and received national publicity, and she was hailed as the mother of the Civil Rights Movement. In her quiet way, she made a stand against the injustice toward her and her people.

I started my career in a hospital laboratory and moved into the pharmaceutical industry. As I traveled up the ladder, there were people against me. Many times, I heard that I received the promotion due to Affirmative Action and not for my skill-set. Because I was overseeing high-profile projects, people had their eyes on me and were ready for me to fail. In those times, I would remember what my grandmother told me when I got my first job: "Whatever it is do the best. Don't let anyone put you down. Working in the hospital, you will be working with doctors. Don't let them talk down to you. You tell them you could be a doctor but God opened a different door for you."

Going from one company to another, my skills increased. I was assigned to start a team in a new therapeutic area. As the therapeutic area became more popular and expanded, my team enlarged. I was an African American woman who created and headed a team of people from different countries working collectively. I had a change in management, and my new boss was impressed by the way that I had created a global team who worked together. But in the corporate environment there were many people who didn't like what I had accomplished.

The company had acquired another company. With the acquisition, there were many changes. Although I still managed my team, I also had additional responsibilities as the assistant site director. The site director left, and it was expected that I would inherit that position. I was in shock when I was told that I would not get the position. The position would be given to a Caucasian woman who had just joined the company six months prior and had never managed a team. When I questioned the head of my department, she indicated that I couldn't lead a team and that I always stood up for the Americans, although it was not an American company. I was flabbergasted. Yes, I spoke up for the people since there was no voice for them regarding how they were treated within the department. Talking further to my boss I realized that I was facing discrimination.

What should I do? I remembered how Zelophehad's daughters went before the court to stake their claim regarding their injustice, and they were heard. I thought of Rosa Parks, who decided that day that she was tired and was not going to give up her seat. If they tried it, I can try it!

The following week I went to the Equal Employment Opportunity Commission (EEOC) to lodge a complaint. EEOC took my complaint and reviewed it. When word got back to my company, I was called into human resources. I was frank with the human resources head about the decision for the site director. I knew it was discriminatory. The person chosen didn't have the managerial skills or communication skills needed for the job, as I had, or the experience. All my performance appraisals had been excellent. There was no legitimate reason why I shouldn't have received the position. But that was not my point. I wanted to expose the injustices that were part of the normal infrastructure of the company. I was taking a stand regardless of the outcome.

What was the outcome? New company policies were implemented regarding discrimination. An 800 number was established to report discrimination. The person who received the site director position was fired due to racist comments that were overheard and reported per the new discrimination policy. I was then asked to take the job as site director, and I declined. By standing up for injustice, God blessed me with a different job that was better than the one I thought I wanted. I stood up for what was right. I tried it.

Questions

1. Would you challenge tradition and injustice? Why or why not?

2. If you were faced with an injustice, what would you do?

3. Have you ever been discriminated against? How did you respond?

Thought for Your Day

As common wisdom holds, every setback sets us up for a comeback.

Closing Prayer

Lord God, as I face the hard times knowing that I am experiencing injustice, I come before you asking for strength and wisdom to prepare me not to give up but to be brave to try and correct the situation. I may fail, but I will try. I may feel that I am alone, but I know you will be right beside me. Amen.

About the Author

Dannita L. Brooker is a director at Sanofi Pharmaceutical in Trial Operations in the Data Expert Services Group. She is married with two children and one grandchild. She is on the ministerial staff of Salem Baptist Church in Jenkintown, Pennsylvania. Her loves are working with the youth, especially to prevent human trafficking, and providing comfort care to the elderly. She is pursuing a Master of Divinity at Palmer Theological Seminary.

NOTE

1. https://www.brainyquote.com/quotes/keywords/trying.html, accessed November 2, 2018.

CONNECTING WITH YOUR STORY

12

Talitha-cumi
Listen to the Child's Cry

DECEMBER PIKE

We need to understand how to allow God to heal our wounds and scars so that we can be whole people. —David G. Evans[1]

Hook Question

Who will be the one to answer your call when you cry out?

Biblical Story: Mark 5:35-43

While he was still speaking, some people came from the leader's house to say, "Your daughter is dead. Why trouble the teacher any further?" But overhearing what they said, Jesus said to the leader of the synagogue, "Do not fear, only believe." He allowed no one to follow him except Peter, James, and John, the brother of James. When they came to the house of the leader of the synagogue, he saw a commotion, people weeping and wailing loudly. When he had entered, he said to them, "Why do you make a commotion and weep? The child is not dead but sleeping." And they laughed at him. Then he put them all outside, and took the child's father and mother and those who were with him, and went in where the child was. He took her by the hand and said to her, "Talitha cum," which means, "Little girl, get up!" And immediately the girl got up and began to walk about (she was twelve years of age). At this they were overcome with amazement. He strictly ordered them that no one should know this and told them to give her something to eat.

Biblical Exposition

There are parents who go to any extent to see that their child is well. If they are sick, they rush to their rooms, go to the store to get medicine, call the doctor, sit at their bedside, and pray on their behalf. They go the distance to ensure their child does not have to suffer. They look for the best medicines, treatments, and doctors. Even if it means going to another town, city, state, or country, they go and use all that they have available to see that their son or daughter is well.

It is comforting to know that there are parents who care about their children and will go to great lengths to take care of their child, but not every child has the necessary attention when they are sick. The sickness can be an illness, physical pain, low self-esteem, depression, neglect, feelings of abandonment, psychological scarring, physical or sexual abuse, and spiritual damage. Sometimes, people do not see that their children are sick and in need of them, to the point that many children are left crying desperately for someone to hear them and give them the help that they need. Many children wrestle with their sickness, carry the weight into adulthood, and commit suicide because no one asked if anything was wrong. Or they run away because no one listens. They never received the help that was needed to get them through their circumstance. But in this Scripture we learn of a father who did not ignore the concerns of his daughter. He pursued Jesus because she was sick and he wanted to see that she was made well.

Jairus was a ruler of the synagogue in a place called Capernaum. He sought after Jesus with considerable faith and was determined to bring Jesus to his home so that his daughter would be cured from her infirmity. He was a father desperate for help and was confident that Jesus was able to deliver her. But word had reached Jairus by a messenger who informed him that his daughter was dead. The faith of Jairus wavered. Jairus was disappointed and overcome by sadness because his hope had failed him. His daughter was dead, and he would have to bury her. If Jesus had been there just a little sooner maybe his daughter would be alive. Hearing about the death of his child broke his spirit, but Jesus reassured him that his daughter was well and that she was just sleeping. Jesus reminded him to have faith.

At Jairus's home, people were found crying, a natural reaction when a loved one or a close friend dies. During Jesus' time, there were women who served as mourners to grieve for families, and they were there mourning the death of Jairus's daughter. In response to Jesus saying that the child was merely asleep, the people laughed and sneered at Jesus publicly, but Jesus wanted to show what happens when you hold to your faith even when belief seems to be impossible. Jesus stopped their procession line because there was life for this sick child. The presence of Jesus became the sign of life in a dead place. Though their hearts were disheartened and their disbelief was measured from what was seen, Jesus intervened and allowed those who were full of faith to witness the miraculous.

Jesus had the heart of believers around him who were trusting in the power of God and not bound in unbelief. The disciples Peter, James, and John were with Jesus and the parents of this sick child. They watched the supernatural happen before their eyes, which was a result of faith. Jesus took hold of this child's hand and spoke life by calling out to her, "Talitha cum," which means, "Little girl, get up!" It was then that the little girl got up from her sleep. It was unspeakable faith that made this little girl well. It was through Jesus that life was reestablished. Physically this child was dead, as it was so for Lazarus, but God had a purpose for this child. To prove that the miracle was real and that she was a living being, Jesus told them to give her something to eat as a sign of life. God had done a miraculous thing in the life of this family—their eyes had seen death take hold of their daughter, but in Jesus the light of life had appeared in their midst. Jesus instructed them not to share what happened in their home because there was always someone finding fault in his actions and trying to have him killed, but eventually word spread about the miracle of this child and people came to believe. This story is a great example of the power of God through Christ and the faith of people who believe.

Personal Story

I have mastered the art of masking. Masking the truth about my spiritual sickness was possible but uncomfortable. No one had seen that my wing was broken from incidents as a child. No one had noticed that I was crying inside deep corners of darkness. No one had seen my tears that dropped on pages as I would write about my brokenness. No one had realized that I held tight to the pillow night after night praying that it would return an embrace to comfort me in my sorrow. No one heard my voice asking myself, "Why did I do this?" I was afraid to walk down the block and walk back through the doors of the place where my innocence had been taken advantage of and choices were made from fear. I just wanted to be left alone.

Looking back, I realized that I was trapped in a web of others' manipulations and schemes, and it left me vulnerable and without a defense. It left me with fear and insecurities and I conceived the feeling of wanting to be alone. It even birthed the discomfort in me to deny my name because it was a reminder of my incident.

I never wanted to go back to the place where the incident happened for fear of my secret being exposed, and this came at the expense of losing a relationship to the one I was supposed to care for. I never returned, and that loved one passed away. I never had an opportunity to say goodbye because of the unwanted fear of being in the presence of the person who had abused me. I learned how to live behind a smile while covering up what was causing me to hurt on the inside. I struggled to understand who I was truly meant to be outside of the taint and bitterness of my attitude and behaviors. I was alone, and no one noticed, and that's when I learned the mechanism to hide. But I did not know the number of years I would be able to get through without exposing the truth.

I was numb, feeling like a target and always looking in the mirror wondering what people saw that made them feel that they could come after me. All I could ever see in the mirror was that little girl feeling ashamed because I felt God had made me someone people could leave broken and mentally abused. I was void of emotion, mentally, physically, and spiritually. I needed a new identity, appearance, and name because what was given to me was stained and blemished by my past.

I hungered for a new birth of life, to be resurrected into that which is true. College served as my personal journey to reinvent myself and learn to become a stronger woman. This is why I cut off my hair and started going by my middle name, which is December. La'Keisha died that day of the incident. I was consumed by fear and afraid that I would be blamed for what happened to me. Though I cried alone, God always found a way to put me to sleep without reminders and to help me rest in his comfort. At first, I thought God did not love me because of the incident, but he rescued me. When God came into my life and touched my hand, December got up. He reminded me that he was always listening and also that my mother did hear my cry. He said, "Remember when you cried out to your mother, she heard your cry and held you without understanding why, but she held those tears that poured from your eyes." Secretly, in that moment, God made me realize that day my mother prayed for me. It was because of her prayers that he came to me in my sickness. He helped me get up by giving me a new start and a new name, December, which I would not come to know until later when I accepted God into my life. I may have died yesterday, but I was reborn again by God giving me a new name.

Questions

1. Who in your life has been there to recognize that you were sick and helped you toward healing?

2. What unresolved matters of your heart are still following you today?

3. What would it take for your scars to be healed and for you to move toward a path of deliverance that will get you to be who God designed you to be?

Thought for Your Day

Always remember that God is listening and hears your cry in those dark places in your life. He is preparing to help you rise from your scarred disposition. Let Jesus take you by your hand and help you stand up.

Closing Prayer

Eternal God, I thank you for being so amazing, loving, and kind. I realize without you, Jesus, I am nothing, but in you my existence lies. Help those who have been broken and are crying out for someone to recognize they are in pain. Their pain has been ignored and not seen by those around them. Let them know that you see them. Cradle their heart with assurance that they will be healed and made whole again. Forgive those that are responsible for creating the scars in others' lives. Awaken awareness in those who did not see and open their hearts to now listen. Strengthen your daughters and your sons to live through their hurt and rise with power to live again. With all power in your hand, God, help them to get up! Amen.

About the Author

December Pike, a native of North Philadelphia, is following in the footsteps of her spiritual father in the ministry, Rev. Dr. James P. Brown, and pursuing a Master of Divinity degree at Palmer Theological Seminary of Eastern University. She is associate pastor at Christian Faith Baptist Church. None of this would be possible without the love and strength of God and family, and especially the support of her loving husband, Anthony Terrell Pike, to whom she has been married for more than ten years. December pursues her passion for the performing arts through the company she founded, Driven By Passion Production, LLC, which serves as a platform to spread the gospel of Jesus Christ but also helps people to establish their voice and speak out through various avenues of artistic expression.

NOTE

1. David G. Evans, *Healed Without Scars: Discovering the Path to Wholeness in Christ* (New Kensington, PA: Whitaker House, 2004), 17.

CONNECTING WITH YOUR STORY

13

Tabitha (Dorcas)

Arise! My Sisters' Keeper

YOLANDA L. WHIDBEE

I never look at the masses as my responsibility; I look at the individual. I can only love one person at a time—just one . . . So you begin. I began—I picked up one person. Maybe if I didn't pick up that one person, I wouldn't have picked up forty-two thousand. . . . The same thing goes for you, the same thing in your family, the same thing in your church, your community. Just begin—one, one, one. —Mother Teresa[1]

Hook Questions

Whom is God calling you to serve in this season? Are you willing to sacrifice your own personal goals to complete God's assignment? Why or why not?

Biblical Story: Acts 9:39-42

So Peter got up and went with them; and when he arrived, they took him to the room upstairs. All the widows stood beside him, weeping and showing tunics and other clothing that Dorcas had made while she was with them. Peter put all of them outside, and then he knelt down and prayed. He turned to the body and said, "Tabitha, get up." Then she opened her eyes, and seeing Peter, she sat up. He gave her his hand and helped her up. Then calling the saints and widows, he showed her to be alive. This became known throughout Joppa, and many believed in the Lord.

Biblical Exposition

The story of Tabitha illustrates divine intervention, dedication to servanthood, love, true friendship, and genuine faith. Tabitha was a well-known seamstress who created and provided free clothing to widows in the port city of Joppa, a city that was known for its beauty and for being a popular place for women who had lost their husbands at sea.[2] In addition, Tabitha was "devoted to good works and acts of charity" (Acts 9:36). Perhaps she assumed financial responsibility for many of those women along with providing them spiritual and emotional support. She was dedicated and committed to serving them.

Tabitha is also known in the Scriptures by the name Dorcas, which is the Greek translation of her first name. The name Dorcas suggests that she was a Hellenist, meaning she was a Jew who lived among the Greeks, spoke the Greek language, and converted to Christianity, a conversion that was sparked by Peter's preaching at Pentecost. At that time, several thousand converted Christians began to spread the gospel to the ports along the Mediterranean.

Throughout Joppa, Tabitha was described as a woman who did good deeds without seeking rewards or recognition. Consistently, she was known for showing others Christ-like love and compassion.

Unfortunately, there came a time when she became seriously ill. As her health declined, several of the widows surrounded her bed and draped it with her handmade tunics and fine garments. Never leaving Tabitha's side, they prayed fervently for a healing miracle. Despite their prayers, Tabitha succumbed to death. Afterward, the widows cried and mourned. The news of her death spread quickly through the land; believers and unbelievers were shocked to learn that she passed away. They could not believe that such a faithful and essential woman of the Christian community was dead. At the same time, some of the women learned that the apostle Peter was nearby in the town of Lydia. As a result, a message was sent to him to come right away.

Luke, the writer of Acts in the Bible, tells the story of Tabitha, a disciple[3] raised from the dead after a prayer from the apostle Peter. In seven short verses, Luke presents Tabitha as a woman who was greatly admired and loved, performed great deeds for Christ, received a miracle that ultimately increased the number of saved souls, authenticated Christianity to nonbelievers, and was shown an act of mercy by God.

This story is a reminder of God's love and goodness toward us. Tabitha led a life that was fully committed to serving others. She had a vision and the courage to do God's work. As a result, hundreds of women's lives were forever changed.

Personal Story

While driving to the youth correctional facility for the first time, there were several questions running through my mind. "What would the girls in the facility think of me? Will they like me? Did I hear clearly from God to come here? What will the outcome be from my first visit?" Once I arrived, I could not help but notice the barbed wire around the building. Although I knew the place was for youth who committed crimes, they were still children in my eyes.

Upon entering the building, I was asked to store all my belongings in the locker. Shortly thereafter, a correctional officer escorted me to the classroom to prepare for my session on personal development. At each turn before arriving at the destination, I heard the clanking of the closing of the doors behind me. Finally, we reached a beautiful and bright classroom where I would be teaching my class. I entered the room and felt a total peace about the space and environment. I knew everything was going to work out.

As the ten young women entered the room with their hands behind their backs, I greeted them one by one. They were shocked that I wanted a hug or a handshake from each one of them. Once I saw their smiles, I knew that I had followed God's instructions and I was in the right place.

For the next several years, I continued to visit the girls staying at the Youth Facility Center. Even though the faces and names changed, there were three consistent needs that never changed. First, each girl wanted to feel loved and appreciated. Second, each girl wanted the opportunity to communicate her thoughts, goals, and future dreams. Third, each girl wanted a mother figure in her life. I was willing to meet all their needs and so much more.

Our weekly meetings centered on discussing various topics such as relationships, self-esteem, career choices, dysfunctional families, molestation, sexual orientation, and abandonment. Eventually, the girls trusted me enough to discuss their religious beliefs or disbeliefs.

In fact, I will never forget the day Michelle (her name is changed for anonymity) decided to stand up in front of the group to sing a gospel song. The Holy Spirit moved so quickly in the room that all the girls, the correctional officers, and I all began to weep. She shared with us how she was a praise dancer at her church and felt like God had abandoned her in prison. Afterward, some of the girls, along with a few of the correctional officers, rededicated their lives to Christ. Once I left the building, I sat in my car and cried. I finally realized why God brought me there.

Initially, I thought my purpose was to share my passion for helping others build their image from the inside out. And what better way than to talk to girls who were from urban cities just like myself? However, I realized that was a very small part of God's plan; the plan was twofold. First, God wanted to introduce me to my God-given assignment, which is empowering women and girls to become whole and to live on purpose. Second, God wanted to give me the daughter I had been praying for and had not conceived yet. I was so focused on praying for God to bless me with a biological daughter, I never considered how God gave me fifty daughters to care for during that time. I loved each of these young ladies so much. They brought me so much joy and unexpected happiness.

As I began to further process my God-given assignment, Tabitha's story resonated with me in so many ways. First, she taught me the importance of wholeheartedly embracing God's plan for my life. Second, I learned to be more open and receptive to the way God answers my own prayers. Third, I learned to be more grateful for the privilege of serving Christ. There are so many women in various countries who are not allowed to pray or serve in public.

Today, my ministry focus continues to be on serving women and young girls. God continues to allow me to be a mother to many. In fact, several of my daughters work closely with me in ministry or have gone into various roles that involve serving others. God resurrected me, like Tabitha, from the dead. Although I was not dead physically, I had dead areas in my life that needed to be resurrected. I'm alive now and excited about the new journey!

Questions

1. Tabitha is an example of a miracle and servant leader. How would you define the term "servant leader"? Do you see yourself as a servant, a leader, or both? Explain.

2. In what ways is God calling you to help others in need (financially, emotionally, spiritually)? When was the last time you helped another person you didn't know?

3. How has Tabitha's story inspired you? How will you in-corporate some of her attributes into your life or ministry?

Thought for Your Day

You have two hands.
One to help yourself, the second to help others.
—Audrey Hepburn[4]

Closing Prayer

Dear God, to whom I give all the honor and praise, reveal to me daily ways to better serve others. Allow me to be trans-parent and authentic at all times. Give me the right words, wisdom, and compassion when speaking to other adults, young people, friends, family members, coworkers, and foes. Continue to teach me how to be more like you. Help me to increase my faith. Amen.

About the Author

Yolanda L. Whidbee is a social entrepreneur, motivational speaker, trainer, and certified image management consultant. She founded Defining YOU Image Management Services, Where First Impressions Are Lasting Ones (www.defininguimagemanagement.com), and PHIERCE Movement, which challenges, empowers, and inspires women and girls to live out their God-given talents and purposes. She holds a Bachelor of Arts degree in commu-nications and journalism. In 2017, she obtained a Master of Theological Studies degree from Palmer Theological Seminary. Today, she continues her life mission of serving others for Christ locally and abroad.

NOTES

1. http://www.searchquotes.com/quotation/I_never_look_at_the_masses_as_my_responsibility%3BI_look_at_the_individual._I_can_only_love_one_perso/12694/, accessed November 2, 2018.

2. "Dorcas, the Woman Full of Good Works," Christian Classics Ethereal Library, http://www.ccel.us/biblewomen.ch19.html, accessed November 2, 2018, based on Harold J. Ockenga, *The Women Who Made Bible History* (Grand Rapids, MI: Zondervan, 1962).

3. The term "disciple" can be found in Acts 9:1-2,36 and Acts 18:24-26. Luke identifies how Tabitha followed God's command to support and care for the poor

and widows in society. Tabitha's story of dying and being bought back to life is one of several miracles performed in the Bible. See T. J. Wray, *Good Girls, Bad Girls of the New Testament: Their Enduring Lessons* (Lanham, MD: Rowman & Littlefield, 2016), 98.

4. https://www.goodreads.com/quotes/580865-as-you-grow-older-you-will-discover-that-you-have, accessed November 2, 2018.

CONNECTING WITH YOUR STORY

14

Sheerah

She's Not Different; She Was First!

SHAWNA M. ADAMS

History is made of firsts. —Monica Haskell[1]

Hook Question

Can God trust you to be first?

Biblical Story: 1 Chronicles 7:23-24

Ephraim went in to his wife, and she conceived and bore a son; and he named him Beriah, because disaster had befallen his house. His daughter was Sheerah, who built both Lower and Upper Beth-horon, and Uzzen-sheerah.

Biblical Exposition

First Chronicles opens up with the genealogy of Israel, beginning with Adam. Usually, only the male descendants are named within biblical genealogy accounts, often leaving any daughters unaccounted for. However, if a woman's name appears, it warrants taking a closer look. Such is the case with Sheerah.

When we come to verse 23, Ephraim had just experienced great tragedy when his sons were murdered. His household had been dismantled, and he and his wife had to start all over again. After having their son Beriah, Ephraim's wife conceived again and they had Sheerah. At first glance, one may move quickly past this brief section of Scripture, but I challenge you to look closer. In a time when women were considered property and were valued primarily for their childbearing abilities, Sheerah had done the seemingly impossible. Though her father's house was torn down, a builder was birthed! Sheerah built three cities, even naming one, Uzzen-sheerah, after herself, which was common for the men who built cities in the ancient world. Uzzen-sheerah means "listen to Sheerah." She could not be denied.

This is the only place in the Bible where Sheerah's name is mentioned, but her work and impact go on for generations. As a side note, this is also the only place where Ephraim's wife, Sheerah's mother, is mentioned. Coincidence? I think not. It's only right to mention the woman who gave birth to the only woman who built three cities in a male-dominated society! Let's be clear about what Sheerah had to do to get this accomplished. She had to teach herself how to design cities because women were not allowed to be educated. She had to hire workers. She had to purchase materials, make the plans, and call the shots. She had to ignore the skeptics, the naysayers, and the haters. She did what no other woman before her had ever done and what every woman after her could follow. Sheerah was a trailblazer. She was a woman with vision, passion, and courage. She was powerful, unstoppable, and anointed by God to do this!

Sheerah's willingness to be the first became a blessing for her family nine generations later, down to her great-great-great-great-great-great-great-great-great-nephew, Joshua. It was greater than just her. Take some time to read Joshua 10 and the account of when God made the sun stand still while Joshua fought the five kings of the Amorites. When you get to verses 9-11, look closely at the cities where the battle was fought and won. Yes, that's right, Beth-horon! Even then, Sheerah was still speaking.

Personal Story

I identify with Sheerah because I, too, am a woman of firsts. I am the first person in my immediate family to get my bachelor's degree, and I am working toward being the first to get a master's degree as well. I was the first woman to become a licensed minister in my church, and I am now the assistant pastor, the first ever, male or female. It has not been an easy road because of the many times I have doubted myself. Some may have the impression that I am a confident, outgoing, strong woman who is never afraid of anything and always has it under control (or at least that is what some have told me). However, the true story is that I second-guess myself all the time. I cringe when my name is called in public. I question decisions and often talk myself out of doing things because of fear that I may not get it right or people may not like it or support it. I'd rather be in the back, managing the execution of the plan, instead of out front as the face of the mission. I would also prefer that the mistakes that I made as "the first" were not always so public, like this next first that I am about to share with you.

I was the first (and only) elder on the clergy staff of my church to have a daughter who got pregnant as a teenager. Yes, an elder in the church, leading the choir, preaching and teaching, and working with the youth department. How did this happen? She was only sixteen! What does this mean for me now? For us? It hit me like a punch to the gut and knocked the wind out of me. I didn't have anyone to help me through the disappointment and the questions. No one could tell me that they had been through it and prepare me for what I should expect. I wasn't ready for the whispers and the looks. I didn't expect that people would stop calling me and inviting me out with the girls. I didn't know that some people would disqualify me from ministry and that others would discredit my anointing. I definitely had no clue that people would strategically and secretly tear my daughter down with their words and leave me to pick up the pieces. No one counseled me on how to minister to a daughter who felt disappointed by God and became indifferent and cold. I guess in some ways, I was in my Ephraim season. Of course, not as severe as losing my children to death, God forbid! But what is worse . . . losing a child naturally or seeing your child gradually die a spiritual death before your eyes and no matter what you do, you can't seem to save them? I believe both instances can cause seemingly unbearable pain.

In God's infinite grace and bountiful mercy, both my daughter and I were restored over time. Through this process, I have come to realize I am not the only Sheerah in this family. There is also a Sheerah in my daughter! Though she was the first teenager to become pregnant in my church, that was not the end of her story, glory be to God. She is now the first medical professional we have in our immediate family, and she is getting ready to become the first licensed practical nurse as well—male or female. And she's not stopping until she becomes a medical examiner. Go, Sheerah! What once was torn down has been built up again, and for a purpose greater than ourselves. It was not just about us.

At some time after my grandson was born, there were other mothers who developed that same look in their eyes that I had as I was grappling with the fact that my baby was having a baby. This time, there was someone they could talk to, someone who understood them and stood with them. Both my daughter and I developed relationships on purpose so that they could know that someone has already walked in their steps and that God brought us through. And God is not selective with God's help, so if God did it for us, then God could do it for them! We were no different. We just were first.

Questions

1. How have you answered God's call in your life to do something that has never been done before?

2. What would you list as "disqualifiers" that start rising up when you think about doing something new or different?

3. What have you built that will impact this world long after you are gone? What do you want to build?

Thought for Your Day

Each of us has a birth date and each of us will have a date of death. It is the dash between them that will matter the most. Don't waste your dash.

Closing Prayer

Most gracious and eternal God, we acknowledge that you have blessed us to be created in your image and likeness. And like you, we have the ability to create. Lord, please help us to trust you and do what you have assigned to our hands. There are lives that are depending on our obedience. May you be pleased with our lives as we surrender our bodies and our will to you, that you will have your way in us. All to Jesus. For your glory. Amen.

About the Author

Shawna M. Adams is a wife, mother, and grandmother who resides in Willingboro, New Jersey. She is the assistant pastor of Word of Life Christian Center in Springfield Township, New Jersey. Shawna is a graduate of Colorado Technical University and is currently pursuing a Master of Divinity at Palmer Theological Seminary. A certified life coach and ordained clergy member, she is in the beginning phase of birthing Developing Diamonds of Destiny, a community program geared toward girls ten to eighteen years of age. It is her desire that through this program, young girls will embrace their worth and live with dignity and without apology.

NOTE

1. Monica Haskell, "Re-invent: Breaking Out the Box to Build the Door; Come Another Way," sermon, Ignite Women's Empowerment Summit, Philadelphia, PA, November 5, 2016.

CONNECTING WITH YOUR STORY

15

The Shunammite Woman
Generosity and the Unexpected

DANNITA L. BROOKER

Some things are so unexpected that no one is prepared for them. —Leo Rosten[1]

Hook Question

What did I do to deserve this?

Biblical Story: 2 Kings 4:8-17

One day Elisha was passing through Shunem, where a wealthy woman lived, who urged him to have a meal. So whenever he passed that way, he would stop there for a meal. She said to her husband, "Look, I am sure that this man who regularly passes our way is a holy man of God. Let us make a small roof chamber with walls, and put there for him a bed, a table, a chair, and a lamp, so that he can stay there whenever he comes to us."

One day when he came there, he went up to the chamber and lay down there. He said to his servant Gehazi, "Call the Shunammite woman." When he had called her, she stood before him. He said to him, "Say to her, Since you have taken all this trouble for us, what may be done for you? Would you have a word spoken on your behalf to the king or to the commander of the army?" She answered, "I live among my own people." He said, "What then may be done for her?" Gehazi answered, "Well, she has no son, and her husband is old." He said, "Call her." When he had called her, she stood at the door. He said, "At this season, in due time, you shall embrace a son." She replied, "No, my lord, O man of God; do not deceive your servant."

The woman conceived and bore a son at that season, in due time, as Elisha had declared to her.

Biblical Exposition

Shunem was a city that was between the cities of Samaria and Carmel, a road that Elisha often traveled. The unnamed Shunammite woman saw Elisha and provided him kindness. The Shunammite woman was a wealthy, married woman who had no children. She extended hospitality to Elisha, whom she recognized as a man of God as he passed through town. In the beginning she provided Elisha food but went further, with the assistance of her husband, by providing Elisha a place or room in her home where he could rest and stay. In this place he could meditate, pray, and be alone.

The Shunammite woman gave freely of herself and didn't ask for anything in return. Her generosity flows from herself to the other person. It is not based on the lack or the neediness of the other person. She showed her desire to give. Her chief gift was recognizing Elisha as a "holy man of God."

Elisha was appreciative of her hospitality and wanted to reward her. He asked her what she would like. Would she like him to use his authority with the king or army commander? She responded by saying that she was happy and content where she was living with her people. How many people would have replied like the Shunammite woman? Most people would give Elisha a list of things that he could give them. She didn't want to climb the ladder of success. She was thankful for what God had provided her and didn't need anything more.

She was a proud and independent woman. She knew the security of a supportive, extended family; she depended on those who knew and loved her; she felt no need for Elisha's influence with king or army commander. Nor did she have any desire to benefit materially from her relationship to Elisha.

Still, wanting to give the Shunammite woman something, he asked his servant Gehazi what could be done for her. Gehazi noticed she had no children. Barrenness was a source of shame and reproach to a wife in ancient Israel. Elisha promised her that she would have a child, a son, by this time next year. She begged Elisha not to raise her hopes. Evidently she had been trying and had not succeeded in having a child. Yet she had a child, a son.

From the story I see the Shunammite woman as caring, giving, going out of her way to help others, and hospitable. Because of the character of the Shunammite woman, she received an unexpected gift. A miraculous gift! A true blessing!

Personal Story

I remember when I was small talking to my mother about her childhood. She was the youngest of eight children and grew up during the Great Depression. During the depression, food was scarce. Although their meals consisted of potatoes, my grandmother always had enough potatoes for the neighbors or anyone who was hungry. My mother was the same; as a teacher she gave herself to her students. When the teachers would go on strike, she would go through the picket lines because the children needed to learn. Giving was instilled in me.

Giving is part of my nature. It gives me pleasure to help other people. Helpfulness is not defined by financial means but by helping people in their need. That was the reason that I became a medical technologist. I wanted to help find a cure for sickle cell anemia. I wanted to stop AIDS. I worked in a hospital so I could help people in their sickness. I joined Bethlehem Baptist Church in the 1990s and was working with the youth. There was a rapid rise in teenagers engaging in recreational drugs. I had recently started a "Just Say No to Drugs" program in the church.

On my way home from church one day I was involved in an accident in which my car was hit head on. I hit my face on the steering wheel. I blacked out for a few minutes but then remember thinking, my car, my car, I just got this car. Back then, there were no safety air bags, and I was stuck in the car with gas leaking. I heard people outside saying "Get her out, because there may be an explosion." I began to say Psalm 23, "The Lord is my shepherd," when I heard a voice saying, "I am not finished with you yet!" I was not expecting to hear those words.

The Jaws of Life were used to get me out of the car. I was put into the ambulance, and I asked where they were taking me. The paramedic looked at me and said I was being taken to Abington, which was a trauma center. Being in the medical field, I knew things were serious if they were taking me to a trauma center. I listened to the paramedics relay my vitals, and they weren't too bad. Upon reaching the hospital, they took me to get a MRI and CAT scan. They needed to give me a dye to check for internal injuries. I overheard them wondering how I survived that horrific crash. They tried to put a tube down my throat to inject the dye, but I kept choking. I said I would drink the dye. They looked at me and said that was not possible. I took the bottle out of their hand and asked for a straw. I drank the dye. There was amazement. What I could do was unexpected to the medical team.

I was in the hospital for five days and out of work for six months. But out of the unexpected car accident came wonderful gifts. Most importantly, I realized again that the God I serve looks after me. Before the accident, I was similar to the Shunnamite woman, in that I had a loving family with a tradition of generosity. That tradition led me to choose a career in which I could help people. And my work with the young people at church was another expression of that generational tradition.

However, God had additional plans for me. After going back to work, I was sought out by a pharmaceutical company for a job. I would be working to develop new drugs to conquer disease: not sickle cell anemia, but cancer; not AIDS, but prevention of heart attacks. Just as the Shunnamite woman didn't expect to have a son, so I didn't expect that my career would take this path. But the intertwined themes of generosity and the unexpected were used by God in the Shunnamite's life and in mine. My unexpected car accident became a wonderful blessing, a way to help others to better health.

Questions

1. What is your response to the saying, "It is better to give than to receive"?

2. What are your expectations in life?

3. How do you respond when something unexpected happens to you?

Thought for Your Day

Giving of yourself freely can render unexpectedness as good, which can result in wonderful blessings. Embrace the unexpected!

Closing Prayer

God, let me continue to give to others even when it sometimes seems not needed. Through my giving, unexpected gifts may be received whether good or bad to the human eye. I thank you for bringing unexpected moments into my life and through them I now become closer to you. I see how you intercede in my life and I am so grateful. Whatever the unexpected, I trust that you mean it for my good. Amen.

About the Author

Dannita L. Brooker is a director at Sanofi Pharmaceutical in Trial Operations in the Data Expert Services Group. She is married with two children and one grandchild. She is on the ministerial staff of Salem Baptist Church in Jenkintown, Pennsylvania. Her loves are working with the youth, especially to prevent human trafficking, and providing comfort care to the elderly. She is pursuing a Master of Divinity at Palmer Theological Seminary.

NOTE

1. Leo Rosten, https://www.brainyquote.com/quotes/authors/l/leo_rosten.html, accessed November 2, 2018.

CONNECTING WITH YOUR STORY

JUNE 2019

Feeling or unappreciated?
You are not alone.

Marginalized, Maligned & Miraculous Women in Scripture explores the stories of women in the Bible who have dealt with these emotions and reveals insights about God and human nature that offer opportunities for us to connect, reflect, and learn. This book will help you:

- Rediscover known and lesser-known Bible stories
- Understand how your story intersects with the stories of others
- Learn from the challenges faced by women, then and now
- Be inspired to live victoriously by faith

Marginalized, Maligned & Miraculous Women in Scripture will help you pursue a faith-filled approach to life's trials. Great for personal inspiration or small-group study, the chapters may be used individually or as one of three 5-week studies.

DEBORAH SPINK WINTERS, MDiv, PhD, is ordained in the United Church of Christ and has served in settled and transitional pastorates. She is Associate Professor at Palmer Theological Seminary of Eastern University and also a Professional Certified Coach. Winters and her husband founded the nonprofit organization *God's Precious Children* to give young people in need a better chance for a brighter future through education. She is also editor of the award-winning title, *Through Her Eyes: Bible Studies on Women in Scripture* (Judson Press, 2016) and contributor to *Who Killed Goliath?* (Judson, 2001), *The Pastor's Bible Study, Vol. 3* (2006), and *The Minister's Annual Manual* (since 2008).

Cover design by Hampton Design Group.

978-0-8170-1797-2 $14.99
51499

www.judsonpress.com